Civil
Liberties

Civil
Liberties

OTHER BOOKS OF RELATED INTEREST

Civil Liberties

Jill Karson, *Book Editor*

Bonnie Szumski, *Publisher*
Helen Cothran, *Managing Editor*
David M. Haugen, *Series Editor*

Contemporary Issues
Companion

GREENHAVEN PRESS
An imprint of Thomson Gale, a part of The Thomson Corporation

Detroit • New York • San Francisco • San Diego • New Haven, Conn.
Waterville, Maine • London • Munich

For more information, contact
Greenhaven Press
27500 Drake Rd.
Farmington Hills, MI 48331-3535
Or you can visit our Internet site at http://www.gale.com

Greenhaven Press anthologies primarily consist of previously published material taken from a variety of sources, including periodicals, books, scholarly journals, newspapers, government documents, and position papers from private and public organizations. These original sources are often edited for length and to ensure their accessibility for a young adult audience. The anthology editors also change the original titles of these works in order to clearly present the main thesis of each viewpoint and to explicitly indicate the opinion presented in the viewpoint. These alterations are made in consideration of both the reading and comprehension levels of a young adult audience. Every effort is made to ensure that Greenhaven Press accurately reflects the original intent of the authors included in this anthology.

LIBRARY OF CONGRESS CATALOGING-IN-PUBLICATION DATA

Civil liberties / Jill Karson, book editor.
    p. cm. — (Contemporary issues companion)
Includes bibliographical references and index.
ISBN 0-7377-2446-3 (lib. bdg. : alk. paper) —
ISBN 0-7377-2447-1 (pbk. : alk. paper)
    1. Civil rights—United States. 2. War on Terrorism, 2001– . I. Karson, Jill.
II. Series.
JC599.U5C5463 2006
323'.0973—dc22
                                            2005051394

Printed in the United States of America

CONTENTS

FOREWORD

In the news, on the streets, and in neighborhoods, individuals are confronted with a variety of social problems. Such problems may affect people directly: A young woman may struggle with depression, suspect a friend of having bulimia, or watch a loved one battle cancer. And even the issues that do not directly affect her private life—such as religious cults, domestic violence, or legalized gambling—still impact the larger society in which she lives. Discovering and analyzing the complexities of issues that encompass communal and societal realms as well as the world of personal experience is a valuable educational goal in the modern world.

Effectively addressing social problems requires familiarity with a constantly changing stream of data. Becoming well informed about today's controversies is an intricate process that often involves reading myriad primary and secondary sources, analyzing political debates, weighing various experts' opinions—even listening to first-hand accounts of those directly affected by the issue. For students and general observers, this can be a daunting task because of the sheer volume of information available in books, periodicals, on the evening news, and on the Internet. Researching the consequences of legalized gambling, for example, might entail sifting through congressional testimony on gambling's societal effects, examining private studies on Indian gaming, perusing numerous websites devoted to Internet betting, and reading essays written by lottery winners as well as interviews with recovering compulsive gamblers. Obtaining valuable information can be time-consuming—since it often requires researchers to pore over numerous documents and commentaries before discovering a source relevant to their particular investigation.

Greenhaven's Contemporary Issues Companion series seeks to assist this process of research by providing readers with useful and pertinent information about today's complex issues. Each volume in this anthology series focuses on a topic of current interest, presenting informative and thought-provoking selections written from a wide variety of viewpoints. The readings selected by the editors include such diverse sources as personal accounts and case studies, pertinent factual and statistical articles, and relevant commentaries and overviews. This diversity of sources and views, found in every Contemporary Issues Companion, offers readers a broad perspective in one convenient volume.

In addition, each title in the Contemporary Issues Companion series is designed especially for young adults. The selections included in every volume are chosen for their accessibility and are expertly edited in consideration of both the reading and comprehension levels of the audience. The structure of the anthologies also enhances accessibility. An introductory essay places each issue in context and provides helpful facts such as historical background or current statistics and legislation that pertain to the topic. The chapters that follow organize the material and focus on specific aspects of the book's topic. Every essay is introduced by a brief summary of its main points and biographical information about the author. These summaries aid in comprehension and can also serve to direct readers to material of immediate interest and need. Finally, a comprehensive index allows readers to efficiently scan and locate content.

The Contemporary Issues Companion series is an ideal launching point for research on a particular topic. Each anthology in the series is composed of readings taken from an extensive gamut of resources, including periodicals, newspapers, books, government documents, the publications of private and public organizations, and Internet websites. In these volumes, readers will find factual support suitable for use in reports, debates, speeches, and research papers. The anthologies also facilitate further research, featuring a book and periodical bibliography and a list of organizations to contact for additional information.

A perfect resource for both students and the general reader, Greenhaven's Contemporary Issues Companion series is sure to be a valued source of current, readable information on social problems that interest young adults. It is the editors' hope that readers will find the Contemporary Issues Companion series useful as a starting point to formulate their own opinions about and answers to the complex issues of the present day.

INTRODUCTION

On September 11, 2001, nineteen men now known to be members of the al Qaeda terror network hijacked four commercial jetliners and slammed two of them into the World Trade Center and one into the Pentagon. The fourth failed to reach its target and crashed into a field in Pennsylvania. More than 2,500 Americans were killed—the largest deadly attack against civilians on American soil. The federal government responded with resolve. In the days that followed, Congress passed bold new policies and laws in the interest of thwarting future attacks. On October 24, Congress approved the USA Patriot Act—short for Uniting and Strengthening America by Providing Appropriate Tools Required to Intercept and Obstruct Terrorism. The Patriot Act produced sweeping changes to existing laws, most notably by increasing the surveillance and investigative powers of law enforcement agencies to help combat the threat of terrorism.

The Patriot Act and other efforts to protect Americans from potentially deadly terrorists have paradoxically generated a national furor over the proper balance between the provision of security and the preservation of a broad swath of civil liberties, from guarantees of freedom of speech, press, and religion, to due process, equal protection under the law, and other limitations on the power of the state to restrict the actions of individuals. Public opinion regarding this complex balance varies widely; many Americans believe that a loss of some measure of freedom is overridden by a gain in national security. Others attest that a truly free society prizes liberties above all else. Still other opinions lie along the spectrum between the two poles.

The current debate—though heightened by the events of 9/11—is not without precedent, however. During past periods of war and crisis, Americans have been required to relinquish some measure of civil liberties. President Abraham Lincoln, for example, suspended habeas corpus during the Civil War and even subjected those who opposed the war, including antiwar activists and draft resisters, to martial law. During World War I, Congress passed the Espionage and Sedition Acts, which gave the government license to deport any alien considered dangerous and also to fine or imprison anyone found guilty of expressing antiwar views or other opinions considered malicious or disloyal. After the Japanese attacked Pearl Harbor during World War II, more than a hundred thousand Japanese Americans and other foreign-born citizens were interned in camps patrolled by armed guards, even though none had been accused of any criminal activity. Following the war, American Communists and others who held views considered subversive were blacklisted as anti-Communist fear gripped the nation. Finally, when America became involved in the extremely controversial

Vietnam War, antiwar protesters were spied on and tried for conspiracy. In all these instances, the curtailment of rights occurred even as the debate over the issues raged.

As in these previous periods of imperiled national security, Americans today are wrestling with a gambit of issues related to their security and personal freedom. Some of the most controversial security measures relate to the treatment of suspected terrorists and the practice of interrogating, arresting, and incarcerating large groups of people based on their nationality or religious affiliations. Other concerns center on freedom of expression as granted in the First Amendment. At issue, for example, is whether an individual's right to voice dissent to the government's antiwar policies may be curtailed. Perhaps some of the most contentious debates, however, center on personal privacy—indeed a lightning rod among civil libertarians.

Many of those concerned with the loss of privacy rights cite the erosion of the Fourth Amendment, which protects Americans against unreasonable searches and seizures. This includes the requirement that law enforcement officers, before conducting an investigation, obtain a warrant from a judge certifying that there is probable cause that criminal activity has taken place. Parts of the Patriot Act, however, weaken this standard. For example, to get a wiretap under the new law officials need only demonstrate "reasonable suspicion" that a person or business is engaged in terrorist or criminal activity—a much lower standard than "probable cause" that a crime has, or will, take place.

Those portions of the Patriot Act that give law enforcement and foreign intelligence agencies more latitude in tracking and monitoring personal communications and other types of transactions are particularly troubling to civil libertarians for another reason: In an age of rapidly advancing technology—officials are equipped with state-of-the-art computers and Internet eavesdropping technology, for example—it is easier than ever for the government to gather information about ordinary, law-abiding Americans who are unconnected to any criminal activity. The sheer breadth of data that the government can clandestinely track—an individual's buying habits, private communications, financial and health records, and Internet accounts—is staggering.

Many worry that these vastly expanded powers are not being balanced with an adequate system of checks and balances. That the Patriot Act, for example, licenses intelligence agencies—part of the executive branch of the government—to gather information without traditional levels of judicial oversight may lead to unbridled executive power and a possible violation of the Fourth Amendment. In the view of the Democratic senator from Wisconsin, Russ Feingold, such unchecked governmental power has the potential to profoundly change society. In a statement to Congress made only a month after the 9/11 attacks, Feingold argued:

Of course there is no doubt that, if we lived in a police state, it would be easier to catch terrorists. If we lived in a country that allowed the police to search your home at any time for any reason; if we lived in a country that allowed the government to open your mail, eavesdrop on your phone conversations, or intercept your email communications; if we lived in a country that allowed the government to hold people in jail indefinitely based on what they write or think, or based on mere suspicion that they are up to no good, then the government would no doubt discover and arrest more terrorists.

But that probably would not be a country in which we would want to live. And that would not be a country for which we could, in good conscience, ask our young people to fight and die. In short, that would not be America.

Preserving our freedom is one of the main reasons that we are now engaged in this new war on terrorism. We will lose that war without firing a shot if we sacrifice the liberties of the American people.[1]

Public awareness of the civil liberty implications of the war on terror is indeed great. To many, however, the enormity of the risks posed by a global terrorist network—a menace that many feel is unparalleled in American history—requires a recalibration between security and personal liberty. In this light, some modest restrictions on privacy rights or other civil liberties are appropriate and necessary. Because America is vulnerable to attack by a stateless, and therefore highly elusive, enemy, many believe that new levels of surveillance are necessary, including the ability to gather critical information about a largely hidden enemy—to investigate, track, monitor, and wiretap suspected terrorists, for example.

Many maintain, too, that the nation's current security measures are not without safeguards and can be implemented in ways that minimize any permanent, adverse effect on personal freedom. Law enforcement, for example, remains subjected to many traditional restraints, albeit modified in some cases. The Patriot Act, moreover, includes a handful of sunset provisions that will expire automatically unless they are renewed by Congress. Supporters claim, too, that actions by past presidents—Franklin Roosevelt when he signed the now infamous Executive Order 9066 that authorized the internment of Japanese Americans during World War II, for example—demonstrate that wartime restrictions on civil liberties, while they may seem unduly harsh at the time, are indeed temporary.

In a 2003 article in *City Journal*, journalist Heather Mac Donald echoes the views of many in her defense of the Patriot Act and other security initiatives that allow the government to confront the threat of terror:

When the War on Terror's opponents intone, "We need not trade liberty for security," they are right—but not in the way they think. Contrary to their slogan's assumption, there is no zero-sum relationship between liberty and security. The government may expand its powers to detect terrorism without diminishing civil liberties one iota, as long as those powers remain subject to traditional restraints: statutory prerequisites for investigative action, judicial review, and political accountability. So far, these conditions have been met.

But the larger fallacy at the heart of the elites' liberty-versus-security formula is its blindness to all threats to freedom that do not emanate from the White House. Nothing the [George W.] Bush administration has done comes close to causing the loss of freedom that Americans experienced after 9/11, when air travel shut down for days, and fear kept hundreds of thousands shut up in their homes. Should al-Qaida strike again, fear will once again paralyze the country far beyond the effects of any possible government restriction on civil rights. And that is what the government is trying to forestall, in the knowledge that preserving security is essential to preserving freedom.[2]

The country faces grave dangers in the aftermath of the attacks on September 11, 2001. Concerns about terrorism remain highly exigent. As Americans continue to debate the state of civil liberties in the post-9/11 environment, a number of highly salient questions remain unanswered: Does the clear and present danger of terrorism justify potential infringements on personal freedoms? Does the very openness of American society benefit those who wish to inflict harm? Will the U.S. law enforcement and intelligence agencies have the requisite power and authority to preempt another terrorist attack—or have they gone beyond the requirements of national security? As the nation attempts to answer these and other questions, preserving its cherished doctrine of civil liberties as it confronts a new kind of enemy will surely remain one of the most important struggles of the twenty-first century. The essays included in *Contemporary Issues Companion: Civil Liberties* examine these and other issues—including freedom of expression, religious liberty, and privacy rights—that are vital to a free and open society, whether in the midst of national crisis or in times of peace and prosperity.

Footnotes

1. Russ Feingold, statement to Congress, October 25, 2001.
2. Heather Mac Donald, "Straight Talk on Homeland Security," *City Journal*, Summer 2003.

CHAPTER 1

THE SOURCE OF CIVIL LIBERTIES

NATURAL LAW PROVIDES THE BASIS FOR CIVIL LIBERTIES

Andrew P. Napolitano

Two opposing theories have traditionally driven the long-standing debate over the source of individual rights. On one side, positivists hold that freedom comes from the government and that rights, therefore, are a creation of the state. Others, including Judge Andrew P. Napolitano, assert that basic human rights and civil liberties derive from "Natural Law"—that is, rights established by God that are immutable and common to all humanity. Freedom of speech and the free exercise of religion, writes Napolitano, are among the natural rights conferred from God; these freedoms cannot be suspended for the sake of a humanly enacted legal system that may be inconsistent with the dictates of Natural Law. Napolitano is Fox News Channel's senior judicial analyst and the author of *Constitutional Chaos: What Happens When the Government Breaks Its Own Laws*, from which the following is excerpted.

For thousands of years philosophers, scholars, judges, lawyers, and ordinary folks have debated and argued over different theories suggesting the sources of human freedom. Though there are many schools of thought addressing these origins, most contemporary legal scholars in the Western world stand behind two principal theories about the origins of freedom: One school, the Natural Law theorists, argues that freedom comes by virtue of being human—from our own nature. The other school, the positivists, argues that freedom comes from the government.

Freedom Comes from God

Natural Law theory teaches that the law extends from human nature, which is created by God. Thus, the Natural Law theory states that because all human beings desire freedom from artificial restraint and because all human beings yearn to be free, our freedoms stem from our nature—from our very humanity—and ultimately from God. St. Thomas Aquinas, the principal modern interpreter of Natural Law, directly contends that because God is perfectly free and humans are created in His image and likeness, our freedoms come from God. The founders held this same basic view.

Such an understanding, that freedom comes not from government but from God, has profound effects on modern jurisprudence. It means, for example, that our basic freedoms, such as freedom of speech, freedom of the press, freedom of religion, freedom of association, freedom to travel, and freedom from arbitrary restraints, cannot be taken away by the government unless we are convicted of violating Natural Law—and the government can only convict us if it follows procedural due process.

Procedural due process means that we know in advance of the violations of Natural Law that the government will prosecute, that we are fully notified by the government of the charges against us, that we have a fair trial with counsel before a truly neutral judge and truly neutral jury, that we can confront and challenge the government's evidence against us, that we can summon persons and evidence in our own behalf, that the government must prove our misdeeds beyond a reasonable doubt, and that we have the right to appeal the outcome of that trial to another neutral judge or judges. This is the only way under Natural Law theory that any of our natural rights can be taken away.

Because free speech is a natural right and can only be taken away after due process, it cannot be legislatively taken away. Thus, Natural Law protects minority rights from incursion by the majority. Under Natural Law, neither Congress nor any state legislatures can declare that freedom of speech no longer exists. Since Natural Law posits that freedom of speech comes ultimately from God, the majority cannot legislate it away.

Natural Law also posits the existence of an independent judiciary with the power to stop a legislature and an executive from interfering with natural rights. Thus, under the Natural Law, if the Congress, for example, made it unlawful to speak out against abortion, or if a state governor stopped Christians and Jews from worshiping, judges can invalidate those acts, even if there were no First Amendment protecting freedom of speech and religion. Because the right to speak and worship as we wish comes from our humanity, not from the government or from the First Amendment, under Natural Law, judges can enforce those rights, notwithstanding the legislature or the executive.

Restricting the Majority

Natural Law would also, of course, prevent the majority from having its way all of the time. For example, a legislature could not by majority vote take property that properly belongs to Person A and give that property to Person B. Why? Because under Natural Law, that legislation would exceed the power of any government by violating the right of Person A to the use and enjoyment of his own property. In fact, the Supreme Court of the United States, back in 1798, addressed just this situation.

The Connecticut Legislature enacted a statute taking property from one citizen and giving it to another. The highest court of the state of Connecticut invalidated the Legislature's act. The U.S. Supreme Court followed and upheld the Connecticut court and, in so doing, ruled that courts have the power to prevent legislatures from intruding upon natural rights because an act of any legislature contrary to the Natural Law cannot be considered a rightful exercise of legislative power. Thus, the court held, there are immutable natural rights that all human beings have that cannot be interfered with by a popular vote or the will of the legislature, but only through due process.

Under Natural Law, legislatures have unwritten limitations imposed upon them, and those limits prevent a legislature, no matter how one-sided the vote and no matter how popular the legislation, from enacting a law which interferes with a natural right. Theoretically, Natural Law proponents would argue that when the people created state legislatures and when the states created the Congress they never gave these legislative bodies the authority to interfere with natural rights.

Critics of Natural Law argue that it is anti-democratic because it prevents the majority from achieving its purpose. Moreover, they contend, since the Natural Law is not written down anywhere in precise legal language, it is impossible to tell what rights are protected by it and what are not. Thus, these critics conclude, a Natural Law theory of government reposes too much power in the hands of judges to decide what rights are natural and what rights are not, and what areas of human behavior may not be regulated or interfered with by the majority, either directly through a popular vote or indirectly through a legislative enactment.

Natural Law also commands certain prohibitions. For example, since taking an innocent life is always wrong, Natural Law commands that murder is unlawful, whether the legislature declares it so or not. Natural Law does, however, recognize that not all rights are natural and some do come from the state. For example, the right to drive a motor vehicle on a government-owned roadway is a right that comes from the state; hence, the government can lawfully regulate it (e.g., requiring a driver's license, limiting speed, etc.) and lawfully take it away (e.g., from habitual drunk drivers).

Government as Giver of Rights

Positivism is more or less the opposite of the Natural Law. Under Positivism, the law is whatever the government in power says it is. Positivism requires that all laws be written down, and that there are no theoretical or artificial restraints on the ability of a popularly elected government to enact whatever laws it wishes. *Carte blanche* all the way.

The advantage of Positivism is that, quite literally, the majority always rules and always gets its way, since there are no minority rights to be protected. Thus, to follow our earlier example, if, under a Positivism theory, a state legislature or the Congress were to enact legislation prohibiting public criticism of abortion, or a state governor were to prevent Christians and Jews from worshiping, so long as the legislature was legally elected and so long as the legislature followed its own rules in enacting the legislation and so long as the legislation proscribed criticism of abortion and authorized the governor's behavior, the prohibition on speech and the interference with the free exercise of religion would be the law of the land, and no court could interfere with it. If rights come from government, they can be repealed by government.

Critics of Positivism have argued that it leads to the tyranny of the majority. These critics remind us that [Adolf] Hitler and his Nazi government were popularly elected, and once in power, under the theory of Positivism, passed all sorts of horrific laws, all of which were *lawfully* enacted. Because there was no Natural Law to protect the minority, these awful laws became the law of the land.

In America, the Declaration of Independence is traditionally referred to as the anchor of our liberties. It is clearly a Natural Law document since in it Thomas Jefferson argues that our rights to life, liberty, and the pursuit of happiness come not from the government, but from our Creator.

The Constitution of the United States, as well, does not grant rights but rather recognizes their existence, guarantees their exercise, and requires the government to protect them. For example, the First Amendment to the Constitution reads in part, "Congress shall make no law respecting an establishment of religion or prohibiting the free exercise thereof; or abridging the freedom of speech. . . ." This clearly implies that the founders recognized that freedom of religious worship and freedom of speech come from some source other than the Constitution. The First Amendment, thus, is not a grant of rights to the people, but a restriction on government, preventing it from infringing on the rights the people already have. It also implies that not only may Congress not interfere with freedom of speech or the free exercise of religion, but Congress must prevent all who act in the name of the government from interfering with them as well. . . .

I, myself, am a strong and fervent believer in Natural Law. The only valid laws are those grounded in a pursuit of goodness. Anything else—like taking property from Person A and giving it to Person B, like silencing an unpopular minority, like interfering with freedom of worship—is an unjust law, and, theoretically, need not be obeyed. St. Thomas Aquinas said only just laws impose an obligation of obedience, because unjust laws are not within the power of the government to enact; and only laws that seek goodness are just. This is the essence of Natural Law. No government may enact laws interfering with our freedoms no matter how popular the enactment.

Civil Liberties Derive from a Consensual Understanding of Injustice

Alan M. Dershowitz

Legal scholar Alan M. Dershowitz is a writer, attorney, and professor of law at Harvard Law School. A longstanding champion of civil liberties, Dershowitz has been at the fore of some of the most important legal debates today. In his book *Shouting Fire: Civil Liberties in a Turbulent Age*, from which the following is excerpted, Dershowitz puts forth his view that the struggle to develop and maintain civil liberties must be understood as an ongoing process, as rights and liberties evolve in response to collective experiences with injustice. The lessons of history, for example, show that when the government establishes—and supports through force—a particular religious ideology, religion is corrupted and individual freedom is curtailed. This experience with injustice, Dershowitz maintains, produced the broad consensus that no individual should be denied the free exercise of his or her own religion; at the same time, past experience continues to inform the contemporary debate over the parameters of religious freedom and the ideal relationship between church and state. Similarly, the shaping of other rights, Dershowitz argues, involves a knowledge of what has failed in the past and a desire to overcome those failures.

The ongoing nature of the righting process does not require that we ignore the wrongs of perfect injustice or allow those who advocate or inflict them to fall back on moral relativism as a justification for absolute morality. There is no possible moral justification for genocide, as evidenced by the fact that no reasoned argument has ever been attempted on its behalf—certainly none has succeeded in the marketplace of ideas over time. Even [Nazi leader Adolf] Hitler and his henchmen tried to hide what they were doing [i.e., the slaughtering of millions of Jews and other minorities] behind euphemisms and evasive rhetoric. Today we have Holocaust deniers but few if any Holocaust justifiers. Indeed, the Holocaust serves as the paradigm of perfect injustice.

Slavery, too, serves as a paradigm of injustice. Yet it had its moral defenders—at a certain time and place in history. The arguments made by these defenders have been soundly rejected by the verdict of history, and not only because the slaveholders lost on the battlefield. Even had the South been victorious [in the American Civil War], the institution of slavery would not have long survived. Economic and moral considerations would have doomed slavery, as it has been doomed in nearly every part of the world.

Slavery, viewed through the lens of experience, has proved to be a paradigm of injustice despite the contemporaneous arguments of its practitioners and defenders. There is no consensus about what perfect justice would be for those who work for others: A fair wage? A share of the profits? Various types of insurance? Reasonable people can and do disagree about perfect economic justice for employees. But every reasonable person now recognizes that slavery was perfect injustice.

The Bottom-Up Approach

In one important respect, therefore, my theory of rights is really a theory of wrongs. It begins with what experience has shown to be absolute injustices: the Crusades, the Inquisition, slavery, the Stalinist starvation and purges, the Holocaust, the Cambodian slaughter, and other unquestionable abuses. It then asks whether the absences of certain rights contributed to these abuses. If so, that experience provides a powerful argument for why these rights should become entrenched. This bottom-up approach builds on the reality that there is far more consensus about what constitutes perfect injustice than about what constitutes perfect justice. If there can be agreement that certain rights are essential to reduce the chances of perfect injustice, that constitutes the beginning of a solid theory of rights. We can continue to debate about the definition of, and conditions for, perfect justice. That debate will never end, because perfect justice is far too theoretical and utopian a concept. But in the meantime, we can learn a considerable amount about rights from the world's entirely untheoretical experiences of injustice. Building on this negative experience, we can *advocate* and *do* basic rights that have been shown to serve as a check on tyranny and injustice. Perhaps someday we will be able to construct a complete theory of rights designed to lead to perfect justice. But since we have had far more experience with perfect injustice than with perfect justice, the bottom-up approach seems more grounded in reality than any top-down approach. It is more modest in its scope, but if it can contribute to a slowing down of the kind of perfect injustice we have experienced in the twentieth century, it will have accomplished a great deal.

Separation of Church and State

Consider the relationship between church and state. Reasonable people can and do disagree about what the ideal relationship between these institutions ought to be: Should governments be entirely neutral toward all religions and toward religion in general? Should the state discriminate against religious speech in the public forum? Should government agencies work with religious institutions on such common goals as the elimination of poverty and the reduction in teen pregnancy and sexually transmitted diseases?

The lessons of history tell us little about the ideal relationship between church and state, though they are relatively clear about what the worst relationship between church and state has been over the years: When the state establishes one particular religion and backs the religious ideology of that church with the military and police power of the government, the experience of history has shown that this relationship corrupts religion and denies citizens freedom of conscience and the free exercise of religious choice. The end results have been crusades, inquisitions, and state-sponsored religious terrorism.

This historical experience has led to a broad consensus—among church leaders, government officials, civil libertarians, and moral philosophers—that government should not establish a particular church and support its particular religious ideology by force; nor should it deny individuals the free exercise of their own religion, even if that religion is deemed to be a "false" one by the majority of the state's citizens.

From this bottom-up conclusion, arguments can and have been made about the content of the rights that should derive from the experiences of the world with the relationship between church and state. Building on these experiences, some argue that a high wall of separation must be placed between the "garden" of the church and the "wilderness" of the state. This powerful metaphor has animated much of the debate about freedom of religion and freedom from religion, which are two sides of the same coin. Strict separationists argue that the wall of separation should preclude governments from supporting religion in general over secularism, even if they support no particular religion. Some believe that it is wrong, in and of itself, for a state to place its imprimatur on religion as such, while others believe that to do so is the first step down the slippery slope of establishing, or preferring, a particular religion. Lurking in the background of this debate are the powerful images of Joan of Arc being burned at the stake, Galileo being imprisoned, Jews being expelled from Spain, Jesus being crucified. These terrible experiences produce a consensus that every person should have the right to choose a particular religion, or no religion, without fear of state-supported persecution. They also inform the debate over how high to build the wall of separation on this basic foundation of experience. This bottom-up approach has the virtue of beginning with a baseline consensus, grounded in the experiences of injustice, and leaving room for reasoned debate beyond that consensus. It need not await the development of a fully articulated theory of the right at issue. It is always a work in progress, building on core experiences and evolving with new experiences.

The Right Not to Be Censored by Government

Another right that can be constructed bottom-up from the injustices of the past is freedom of speech. There is considerable controversy over the positive theory of free speech: Does the so-called marketplace of ideas really work, especially in a world in which the marketplace is heavily skewed in favor of those who can afford to buy time in the media? The experiential case *for* freedom of speech is not nearly as compelling as the case *against* governmental censorship. Societies in which citizens do not choose to speak out publicly on a range of issues can be good and decent, if somewhat boring, places. There is far less public controversy in some Scandinavian countries than in the United States and some other European countries. Yet there is no less freedom, justice, or fairness in these "quiet" places than in more "noisy" venues.

The same cannot be said about societies in which a system of governmental censorship determines what a citizen may say, write, read, or hear. It has been said that governments that begin by burning books end up by burning people. This may overgeneralize the historical record, but it makes an important point: a regime of governmental censorship often entails other evils, such as informers, searches, loyalty oaths, coercion, and torture.

Even without these additional adverse consequences, the dangers inherent in governments' dictating what their citizens can read, see, and hear have been demonstrated by the historical record. The road to perfect injustice has often been paved by governmental control over all sources of information. Based on this experience with injustice, we have developed a consensus, not necessarily regarding the *virtues* of free speech but concerning the *vices* of a regime of governmental censorship, especially prior restraint. Our Bill of Rights does not entrench a general right of free expression: corporations, universities, churches, families, and other nongovernmental entities need not allow their members to speak freely. Only the government may not "abridge" the freedom of speech by state censorship. Building on that core right, which grows out of our experiences with injustice, we are involved in a never-ending debate about the appropriate scope of that right: Should it be permissible for a government to impose spending limitations on the exercise of free speech by the wealthy in order to level the playing field for the less affluent? Should it be permissible for a government to censor certain specified genres of speech—for example, pornography, racism, and historical untruths—in the interests of promoting equality? These and other proposed exceptions are debatable among reasonable people. Some opponents of such exceptions argue, in similar fashion to those who argue for a high wall of separation between church and state, that any governmental power to censor is wrong in and of itself, while others contend that it is the first step toward a full regime of censorship. Again, we need not await the development of a fully articulated positive theory of free expression. We can build from the bottom up, based on the widespread consensus against governmental regimes of censorship that have contributed to the experiences of perfect injustice in the past.

The late justice Robert Jackson, in the middle of the horrors of the Second World War, drew some basic conclusions about rights from these experiences, in words with which few will disagree:

> If there is any fixed star in our Constitutional constellation, it is that no official, high or petty, can prescribe what shall be orthodox in politics, nationalism, religion, or other matters of opinion or force citizens to confess by word or act their faith therein.

This is a solid experiential foundation on which to build a more complete theory of expressive rights, as well as other fundamental rights.

The Constitution Does Not Grant Civil Liberties, It Only Protects Them

Jacob G. Hornberger

Jacob G. Hornberger is the founder and president of the Future of Freedom Foundation, a nonprofit organization that promotes limited government and individual liberty. In the following selection, which originally appeared in the foundation's *Freedom Daily*, Hornberger attempts to dispel what he calls the "common misconception" that people's rights of life, liberty, and property come from the Constitution. According to Hornberger, a careful examination of the Constitution reveals that the founding fathers did not grant specific rights to anyone. Rather, the Constitution called the government into existence and delegated to it very specific powers—to protect law-abiding people, for example. At the same time, it expressly forbade the government from interfering in a wide ambit of personal freedoms, including the right to procedural due process or the right to express unpopular views.

One of the most common misconceptions in the United States is that people's rights come from the Constitution. Without the Constitution, it is believed, people wouldn't have such rights as freedom of expression and religion. People should be grateful to the Founding Fathers, it is said, for establishing the vehicle by which people could have such rights as life, liberty, and property.

Nothing could be further from the truth.

In order to determine the true purpose of the Constitution, it is necessary to first ask some fundamental questions. What is the meaning of human freedom? What is the legitimate role of government in a society? What is the relationship between freedom and government?

What does it mean to be free? Some people say that freedom means freedom of expression. As long as people are able to write letters to the editor, deliver speeches, contact their congressman, write articles, and otherwise express their complaints, they are still free.

But the problem with this limited interpretation of freedom is that theoretically a slave could then be free. For example, consider a slave in the Old South. Imagine that the law or the Constitution had guaranteed him the right to complain about his condition. He could write letters and articles, give speeches on the plantation, and even complain to his congressman about his plight.

Would all that mean the slave was now free?

Other people say that freedom means the right to participate in the electoral process. As long as a person can vote, that means he's free. But again, let's imagine that slaves on the plantation were accorded the right to vote. Suppose that on election day, someone from the state election office would visit the slaves' place of work, order them to line up, and then have them vote for the candidates of their choice. Why, even imagine that they had the right to elect their taskmasters on the plantation.

Would all this democracy mean that the slaves were free?

Freedom means religious liberty, it is said. As long as a person is not forced to attend or support a church, that means he's free. Thus, if slaves were free to attend their own religious services on the plantation or even avoid religious services altogether, they would be considered free under this meaning of freedom.

The Development of the Concept of Freedom

Actually, there are many facets to the meaning of freedom, and man's understanding of the concept has evolved over the centuries and continues to do so to the present date.

Many centuries ago, people considered freedom to mean simply the absence of physical restraint. As long as a person wasn't in jail, for example, he was considered free.

Gradually, people began realizing that freedom means much more than that. It also means freedom of religion and the press. The right to peacefully assemble. To associate with people of one's choice. To petition government for redress of grievances.

In the area of civil liberties, freedom came to encompass procedural due process, including protection from unreasonable searches and seizures and the right to an attorney in criminal cases, to cross-examination of government witnesses, and to a jury trial.

During the 1800s, the people of the United States raised the meaning of liberty to the highest level ever by developing the importance of economic liberty. To our American ancestors, freedom meant more than intellectual, religious, and civil liberty. It also meant the right to engage in economic enterprise freely, to freely enter into mutually beneficial economic exchanges with others, to accumulate the fruits of those exchanges, and to decide how to dispose of their income and property.

In other words, unless a person was able to freely engage in all these activities, he could not consider himself truly free. In fact, compare the aspects of economic liberty to those whom our ancestors excepted from freedom—the slaves on the plantations. They were obviously not free to engage in economic enterprise freely, exchange freely with others, accumulate wealth, and freely dispose of their wealth. They were required by law to work full time for the benefit of others.

In fact, the greatest reward that the state could bestow upon a slave in the Old South was to set him free—which would mean that he would be on his own, free to engage in all these economic activities. But at the same time, freedom would mean that he would not have guaranteed work, food, and housing on the plantation.

Nineteenth-century American lawyers played a major role in the development of the concept of economic liberty. Ultimately, as a result of their efforts, the U.S. Supreme Court would interpret economic liberty, including liberty of contract, as substantative due process (as opposed to procedural due process).

This meant that economic liberty would be immune from government control, in much the same way that intellectual liberty and religious liberty were. Unfortunately, during the 20th century, the Supreme Court, reversed course and resorted to the age-old concept of economic enslavement that has gripped people throughout time.

Most people throughout history have believed that their right to freedom comes from government, but America's Founders believed otherwise. They believed that liberty precedes government.

That is, in the absence of government, people are born with certain natural rights. These include the rights to engage in economic enterprise, especially as a way to sustain one's life, to improve one's condition by trading with others, to keep the fruits of those trades, and then to pursue happiness through the disposition of those fruits.

So, why do people need government? Because there are always antisocial, violent people in life, people who are not interested in engaging in economic enterprise (Read: work) but find it more attractive to simply steal the fruits of other people's earnings. Or people who decide, for whatever reason, to unjustly kill another person or interfere with other people's pursuit of peaceful activity.

So what do peaceful people in society do about such violent, antisocial people?

The Role of Government

They form a government that has a monopoly of force to suppress the wrongdoer. And the majority, who presumably are people who are not interested in murdering, robbing, stealing, raping, and the like, set forth the conditions under which government shall have the power to use its force.

Without government, society is besieged by the violent marauder who cares nothing about people's rights. With government, the violent marauder can be suppressed and punished.

Thus, that's a primary purpose of government—to protect peaceful, law-abiding people from the violent acts of the small minority of violent people in society. This is one major reason that government is called into existence by the people.

But there's obviously one big problem: What happens if government's use of force causes more destruction than would be seen in the absence of government? For example, it would be difficult to imagine that in the absence of a government in the 1930s and 1940s, the German people would have killed as many people as the Nazi government did.

That's the purpose of a constitution—to limit the powers of a government so that it does not abuse its monopoly over the use of force and possibly even make the situation worse than if there had been no government at all.

"But that can't happen in a democracy because the majority rules," people say. Our Founders recognized otherwise. They understood that sometimes people, acting in a mob, could be more dangerous and destructive than violent, antisocial individuals. That's why the first ten amendments to the Constitution expressly protect us from the potential tyranny of majority rule.

Therefore, accepting that government is needed to protect people from violent, antisocial persons in society, the issue becomes: How do people protect themselves from government itself?

The Role of a Constitution

They do so with a constitution, which expressly delegates to the government specific and well-defined powers and which also expressly restricts the powers of the government. The goal is, of course, to ensure the widest ambit of liberty for peaceful, law-abiding people.

Therefore, a constitution has a dual purpose: to call into existence a government but, at the same time, to limit the powers of that government. After all, theoretically it would be possible to call into existence a government with the power to "do the right thing." But "the right thing" in the minds of some people is: Force them to go to church, make them read only "proper" literature, require a license to engage in economic enterprise, and coerce people to share their wealth with others.

A careful reading of the U.S. Constitution reveals that it does not grant any rights to anyone. Instead, while setting up the federal government, the document (including the first ten amendments) also expressly prohibits the government from interfering with various aspects of human freedom.

In summary, then, people have a right to be free. This entails much more than not being in jail. It involves the right to freely engage in intellectual, religious, and economic activity without interference from others, as long as conduct remains peaceful. Freedom cannot consist of the right to violently interfere with other people's peaceful choices.

What happens when a government becomes so bad and abusive that the situation is actually worse than it would be in the absence of government?

That question was answered in the Declaration of Independence. In that document, Thomas Jefferson pointed out that in such instances, the citizenry have the right to alter or abolish their government and to institute new government. In the context of the U.S. Constitution, this means that people have a right to alter or amend their Constitution when their government goes astray or even to revolt and establish a new government.

Freedom cannot be achieved in the absence of government, and government is necessary to ensure freedom. The problem, of course, is how to maintain government within its legitimate role protecting freedom rather than destroying it. That's the role of a constitution. In the absence of a constitution, properly enforced, freedom is impossible.

CHAPTER 2

SEPARATION OF CHURCH AND STATE

THE FIRST AMENDMENT INTENDS THE SEPARATION OF CHURCH AND STATE

Albert Menendez and Edd Doerr

At issue in the current debate over the separation of church and state is the clause of the First Amendment that states that Congress shall "make no law respecting an establishment of religion, or prohibiting the free exercise thereof." According to many civil libertarians, the founding fathers clearly intended the separation of government and religion in the interest of promoting religious liberty and democratic values in general. In the following viewpoint, Albert Menendez and Edd Doerr examine the historical basis for this view: Citing the work of John Milton, Thomas Jefferson, and others, the authors examine how the concept of separation evolved in America during the seventeenth and eighteenth centuries—and how religious liberty became an integral part of American culture. Menendez is the associate director and Doerr is the president of Americans for Religious Liberty.

We hear a great deal about separation of church and state today, especially from those who revile the concept, regard it as somehow foreign or un-American, and want to replace it with some form of official or unofficial cooperation between religious groups and government. So it is now time to take a fresh look back at how the concept evolved and became an essential part of American law and culture.

The concept of separation evolved during the seventeenth and eighteenth centuries from two movements.

The Enlightenment view, so ably expounded by people like John Milton and John Locke, emphasized liberty of conscience in religious matters and implied a minimum of state involvement with religion.

As early as 1644 Milton affirmed in his *Areopagitica*, "Give me the liberty to know, to utter, and to argue freely according to conscience, above all liberties." In 1689 Locke observed in *A Letter Concerning Toleration*, "I esteem it above all things necessary to distinguish exactly the business of civil government from that of religion and to settle the just bounds that lie between the one and the other." Roger

Williams, religious reformer, gadfly, and founder of the Rhode Island colony, was a contemporary of Milton and Locke. In his 1644 book, *The Bloudy Tenet of Persecution*, Williams wrote, "Enforced uniformity confounds civil and religious liberty and denies the principles of Christianity and civility. No man shall be required to worship or maintain a worship against his will."

Then there was what can roughly be labeled the antiestablishment or disestablishment movement, which began among religious dissenters in the American colonies. This movement sought a purely voluntary religion and crystallized its sentiments in opposition to obligatory ties to an established church. Writes historian William G. McLoughlin, "The history of separation of church and state in Massachusetts from 1692 to the Great Awakening is a story of how the Quakers, Baptists, and Anglicans fought, each in their own way, to establish their right to exemption from paying compulsory religious taxes for the support of the Congregational churches."

A Guaranty of Religious Liberty

Hence, a kind of rationalist-pietist alliance achieved the legal recognition of separation as a vital guaranty of religious liberty. McLoughlin says, "There were two or perhaps three different theories of church-state relations at work among those who advocated separation. The view of [James] Madison, [George] Mason, and [Thomas] Jefferson, as expressed in the great debates over this issue in Virginia, has been assumed to be the primary or fundamental one. Most historians and most recent decisions of the U.S. Supreme Court have drawn on the eloquent and logically consistent reasoning of these learned, latitudinarian Anglicans and deists in defining the traditions of separation. . . . The pietists [a religion that stresses personal piety over organized religion] wanted separation in order to keep religion free from interference by the state. The deists [those who practice a rationalist religion that rejects supernatural revelation] wanted separation in order to keep the state free from interference by religion."

This new understanding of church-state relationships won the support of conservative Baptists, such as Isaac Backus, and liberal humanists, such as Thomas Paine. In his 1773 *Appeal to the Public for Religious Liberty* Backus proclaimed, "Religious matters are to be separated from the jurisdiction of the state not because they are beneath the interests of the state, but, quite to the contrary, because they are too high and holy and thus are beyond the competence of the state." Just three years later Thomas Paine reached a similar conclusion in *Common Sense* when he observed, "As to religion, I hold it to be the indispensable duty of government to protect all conscientious professors thereof, and I know of no other business which government has to do therewith."

Between 1775 and 1791 Americans conceived, fought for, and established a new nation. This new nation, as Thomas Jefferson explained in the Declaration of Independence in 1776, was based on the proposition that all persons are created equal, that they have inherent natural rights to "Life, Liberty, and the Pursuit of Happiness," that "to secure these rights, Governments are instituted among Men, deriving their just powers from the consent of the governed," and that "it is the Right of the People to alter or abolish" any form of government that does not secure the rights of the people.

In 1787, having won by force of arms their independence from Great Britain, representatives of the states met in Philadelphia to create a workable federal government. They planned a limited government of delegated powers only; one which implemented, though imperfectly, the principles of the Declaration. The purposes of the new government, spelled out in the Preamble to the Constitution, were to "establish Justice, insure domestic Tranquility, provide for the common defense, promote the general Welfare, and secure the Blessings of Liberty to ourselves and our Posterity."

The people of the United States had fought six long years for their political independence, and had also in the several states deliberately moved away from the European and earlier colonial models of church-state union and religious intolerance. As a result their representatives in Philadelphia carefully avoided granting the new government any power or authority whatever to meddle with or involve itself with religion. The Constitution they created limited the federal government to purely secular matters. Further, Article VI of the Constitution, in an important departure from colonial practice, stipulated that "no religious test shall ever be required as a qualification to any office or public trust under the United States." The same article also prohibited mandatory oaths, by providing that all members of the executive, legislative, and judicial branches "both of the United States and of the several states" may be bound by either an "oath or *affirmation*" (italics supplied) to support the Constitution.

Thus the Constitution implies the principle of separation of church and state. This its principal architect, James Madison, and the Declaration's author, Thomas Jefferson, had championed and had seen enacted into law in Virginia only a short time before the Philadelphia convention. Indeed, Madison had spelled out the rationale for the separation principle in his 1785 *Memorial and Remonstrance*, a short treatise aimed at securing passage of Jefferson's Act for the establishment of Religious Freedom in the Virginia legislature.

The Bill of Rights

Although the new Constitution represented the greatest single advance in the long evolution of democracy and freedom, it was viewed by many, including Jefferson, as containing a serious defect, the absence of an explicit bill of rights. Ratification of the new charter of government hinged on the promises of politicians to add a bill of rights to the Constitution as soon as possible; promises carried out by the First Congress, which in 1789 proposed amendments which were ratified by the states by the end of 1791.

The First Amendment provides that "Congress shall make no law respecting an establishment of religion, or prohibiting the free exercise thereof."

President Jefferson, writing to the Danbury Baptist Association in Connecticut on January 1, 1802, in a letter in which he had given a great deal of thought and which he cleared through his attorney general, stated, "I contemplate with sovereign reverence that act of the whole American people which declared that their legislature should 'make no law respecting an establishment of religion, or prohibiting the free exercise thereof' thus building a wall of separation between church and state."

From that day until this most Americans and their courts of law have agreed with Jefferson's view, and the separation principle has enabled the United States to achieve the world's highest levels of individual religious freedom, religious pluralism, and interfaith peace and harmony. The history of our country and of the world has amply demonstrated the inestimable value of this principle and the genius of those who developed it.

Church-state separation, incidentally, complements and supplements those other great American contributions to freedom and democracy; the principles of federalism, separation of powers, and checks and balances. All of these arrangements are intended to block excessive concentrations of power.

Separation continues to inform the judicial process when religious questions reach the civil jurisdiction. As early as 1872 the U.S. Supreme Court affirmed this: "The structure of our government has, for the preservation of civil liberty, rescued the temporal institutions from religious interference. On the other hand, it has secured religious liberty from the invasion of the civil authority."

State courts have been no less vigorous in affirming this separation. In 1918 the Iowa Supreme Court observed, "If there is any one thing which is well settled in the policies and purposes of the American people as a whole, it is the fixed and unalterable determination that there shall be an absolute and unequivocable separation of church and state." And in 1938 the New York Supreme Court declared, "In all civil affairs there has been a complete separation of church and state jealously guarded and unflinchingly maintained."

It should come as no surprise that 35 state constitutions explicitly affirm separation of church and state, and the others do so implicitly. Even the Commonwealth of Puerto Rico's constitution, approved by the U.S. Congress in 1952, states firmly, "There shall be complete separation of church and state."

Several American theologians and historians have acclaimed the implementation of church-state separation as a major advance for human freedom. James Luther Adams, a Unitarian theologian at Harvard Divinity School, wrote, "The demand for the separation of church and state and the emergence of the voluntary church represent the end of an old era and the beginning of a new one. The earlier era had been dominated by the ideal of 'Christendom,' a unified structure of society in a church-state. In the new era the voluntary church, the free church, no longer supported by taxation, was to be self-sustaining; and it was to manage its own affairs. . . . In this respect the freedom of choice was increased. The divorce of church and state and the advent of freedom of religious association illustrate this type of increase in freedom of choice."

Leo Pfeffer, the dean of church-state lawyers, observed a quarter century ago, "Before the launching of the American experiment, the concept of religious liberty and the separation of church and state was—for all practical purposes—unknown. The experiment was a uniquely American contribution to civilization and one that the other countries of the world in increasing numbers have emulated and are continuing to emulate. The principle of separation and freedom was conceived as a unitary principle. Notwithstanding occasional instances of apparent conflict, separation guarantees freedom, and freedom requires separation. The experiences in other countries indicate clearly that religious freedom is most secure where church and state are separated, and least secure where church and state are united."

A century ago evangelical historian Phillip Schaff reflected on the meaning of separation in his 1888 book, *Church and State in the United States*. He wrote, "The relationship of church and state in the United States secures full liberty of religious thought, speech, and action. Religion and liberty are inseparable. Religion is voluntary and cannot be forced. The United States furnishes the first example in history of a government deliberately depriving itself of all legislative control of religion."

As they have enforced separation of church and state, the courts have come under increasing attack in recent years from certain sectarian special interests. But Americans who know something about their history and who cherish religious freedom should applaud these decisions. Our courts are reaffirming the best of our traditions when they preserve a central principle of American jurisprudence.

THE FIRST AMENDMENT DOES NOT INTEND THE SEPARATION OF CHURCH AND STATE

Jeff Jacoby

In the following selection Jeff Jacoby argues that the U.S. Constitution was written by men who recognized the importance of religion to their new nation. America's founders believed that they were acting under the direction of God when they established the United States, and that same feeling of divine guidance informed their writing of the U.S. Constitution, including the First Amendment. Jacoby contends that those who say the First Amendment, which prohibits an establishment of religion, was intended to remove religion from the political life of the country are wrong. He points out that on the same day the First Amendment was approved by the First Congress, the Congress also passed the Northwest Ordinance, which acknowledged the importance of religion to good governance.

Michael Newdow, the atheist who went to court to get the Pledge of Allegiance declared unconstitutional, spent his 15 minutes of fame [in the summer of 2002] asserting that the Founding Fathers would have cheered his campaign against the words "under God."

"He is confident," the *Washington Post* reported, "that the framers of the Constitution would have supported his view, noting that they did not mention God in the nation's founding document." He had earlier made the same claim on television, telling Katie Couric, "There is no reference to God in the Constitution. It's striking . . . that it is missing."

God and the Constitution

As it happens, there *is* a reference to God in the Constitution, a specifically Christian reference: "Done in Convention by the Unanimous consent of the States present," the final sentence begins, "the Seventeenth Day of September in the *Year of our Lord* one thousand seven hundred and Eighty seven. . . ." If the Framers were as determined as Newdow seems to think they were that the political system they were crafting be sanitized of any hint of God, surely they would have found a different way to date their document.

In fact, the last thing the founders of the American republic wanted was a public square from which every reference to God was removed. "Americans of the founding generation appealed without flinching to the undeceivable Judge of all consciences," Michael Novak writes in *On Two Wings*, his stirring . . . book on the centrality of religion to American nationhood, "precisely because they believed they had formed a covenant with Him, in the name of His most precious gift to the universe, the liberty of the sons of God."

Trying to make sense of the creation of the United States with reference only to its Enlightenment underpinnings is, in Novak's metaphor, "to cut off one of the two wings by which the American eagle flies." The philosophy of liberty developed by thinkers such as John Locke and Charles Montesquieu was crucial in shaping the ideas later embodied in the Declaration of Independence and Constitution, but it was only half the story. Religion was the other half.

The Pledge of Allegiance wasn't written until late in the 19th century; the phrase "under God" wasn't added until halfway through the 20th. But the 18th-century men who led America into revolution and independence never doubted for an instant that America is a "nation under God."

For freedom, they believed, was what God intended for His human creatures—the freedom to be faithful to God's purposes and to follow the course He had set out in the Bible. In fighting for liberty and in establishing a republic, they were advancing God's vision for mankind; they saw their young nation as a new Israel, a people chosen by the Almighty and liberated with His help so they might build a society worthy of His ideals.

"I always consider the settlement of America with reverence and wonder," John Adams wrote in 1765, "as the opening of a grand scene and design in Providence for the illumination of the ignorant and the emancipation of the slavish part of mankind all over the earth."

It was a point others would make again and again, both in the years leading up to the war with England, and long after that war was won.

In an influential sermon in 1776, the Rev. John Witherspoon—James Madison's teacher at Princeton and a leading member of the Continental Congress—argued that God's hand could be discerned in the gathering storm and in the chain of events that had led to it. "It would be a criminal inattention," he said, "not to observe the singular interposition of Providence hitherto, in behalf of the American colonies."

At a very different moment 11 years later, reflecting on the remarkable unanimity achieved by the Constitutional Convention—a body that should have been riven by bickering factions—Madison likewise saw divine intervention.

"It is impossible," he wrote in Federalist No. 37, "for the man of pious reflection not to perceive in it a finger of the Almighty hand which has been so frequently and signally extended to our relief in the critical stages of the revolution."

God and the First Amendment

But a nation under God is not just a nation whose destiny has been guided by Heaven. It is a nation, the Founders insisted, that never forgets that there is, as the Declaration put it, a "Supreme Judge of the World" who holds men and women responsible for their deeds. To them, awareness of God was not optional—not if American liberty and republican government were to succeed.

"Of all the dispositions and habits which lead to political prosperity, religion and morality are *indispensable* supports," George Washington avowed in his Farewell Address. It was a conviction he shared with most of his contemporaries.

Indeed, the idea that government support for religion is incompatible with the First Amendment would have struck the Framers of that amendment as ludicrous. On the same day the First Congress approved the constitutional language prohibiting "an establishment of religion," it also passed the Northwest Ordinance, which authorized a government for the territory north of the Ohio River. "Religion, morality, and knowledge, being necessary to good government and the happiness of mankind," the law specified, "schools and the means of education shall forever be encouraged."

Even Thomas Jefferson, though skeptical of much that he read in the Bible, believed that inculcating Judeo-Christian virtue was essential for America's political well-being. For that reason, he not only made a point of attending church, but used federal funds to support the weekly religious services held in the capitol and other government buildings.

Much has changed in the last [two centuries], but the health of our political institutions still depends on our ethics and religion. The men of 1776 have long since gone to their reward, but it remains our responsibility to preserve today what they envisioned so long ago: one nation under God, with liberty and justice for all.

Public Expressions of Faith Do Not Violate the Constitution

Alan Sears

In the following viewpoint, Alan Sears decries recent attempts to remove the words "under God" from the Pledge of Allegiance. To Sears, the pledge's reference to God and similar affirmations of faith signify the religious liberty that made America a great country. Sears avers that the religious worldview held by many of the nation's founding fathers confirm his view that America is a historically Christian nation; jurisprudence that mandates a complete separation of church and state, then, eradicates the intent of the founders—and the rich American tradition of religious expression. Alan Sears is the president and CEO of the Alliance Defense Fund, a legal alliance that defends religious freedom.

Far more than two simple words are at stake as we await an opinion from the United States Supreme Court in *Elk Grove Unified School District v. Newdow*. The court is weighing whether the words "under God" should be removed from the Pledge of Allegiance. [The Supreme Court ruled that Michael Newdow could not challenge the Pledge of Allegiance.]

To put this debate in proper context we must first recall that in this Republic, the pledge's recitation is a voluntary act of citizenship that no one can be compelled to utter against their conscience.

Public expressions concerning the importance of religion are as old as the Republic, and have historically been viewed as affirmations of faith that made America great. It has been understood from the beginnings of this nation that an essential part of religious liberty is the freedom for our citizens to individually and corporately acknowledge their faith in and dependence upon God. And there is nothing more American than to recognize our nation's dependence upon God—and acknowledge that all of our laws and national acts are under His authority—through the words of the Pledge.

From American history we know that "under God" captures the bedrock worldview of the Founding Fathers who made America. The

Alan Sears, "FIRST-PERSON: The Pledge: What Would Washington Say?" www.alliance defensefund.org, March 23, 2004. Copyright © 2004 by Alliance Defense Fund. All rights reserved. Reproduced by permission.

view of religion held by the majority of the founders was profoundly exhibited in the life of General George Washington. When he received a copy of the Declaration of Independence from the Continental Congress, Washington ordered that "The Colonels or commanding officers of each regiment are directed to procure Chaplains accordingly; persons of good Characters and exemplary lives."

What does the Declaration say about the founders' worldview? God is the Creator and the source of liberty ("all men are endowed by their Creator with unalienable rights"), God is the law giver ("law of nature and of nature's God"), God is the ultimate judge ("the Supreme Judge of the World"), and God is the king above all earthly rulers, the Sovereign ("Divine Providence").

At his presidential inauguration, Washington took the oath of office with his hand on a Bible opened to Genesis 49 and 50, and added the words repeated by every president since, "So help me God." He told his audience that, "It would be peculiarly improper to omit, in this first official act, my fervent supplications to that Almighty Being who rules over the universe, who presides in the councils of nations."

It's not hard to imagine President Washington being outraged at the attempt to remove "under God" from the pledge. He'd probably want to know why it took us until 1954 to add those vital words.

Faith Under Attack

American traditions of expressing our founders' kind of faith have been under attack from the ACLU [American Civil Liberties Union] and its allies for decades. The legal (and public opinion) blitzkrieg has demolished all too many public expressions of faith: crosses, Ten Commandments monuments, nativity scenes, and even Christmas trees. Too many communities in the country can tell a story of an intimidating ACLU demand that a much-beloved expression or tradition be expunged from public life because of the so-called "separation of church and state."

The ACLU's version of the "separation of church and state" cannot be allowed to continue long enough to become an American tradition itself. We can still repel the forces of secularism and their assault on our faith traditions and religious liberty. We can do that in part by remembering to pray that the Supreme Court votes with the side of the angels and keeps "under God" in the pledge.

On some deep level the majority of Americans understand the danger of erasing those words from the Pledge and the further precedent for chaos such a decision would create in the drive to eradicate our heritage. A recent poll found that 89 percent of Americans support keeping "under God" in the Pledge of Allegiance. And a clear majority know there is no constitutional violation here, despite what two judges on the Ninth Circuit—or even five justices on the Supreme Court—might say to the contrary.

People of Washington's era—those who wrote the First Amendment —understood "establishment of religion" far differently than today's judges. For the founders, an establishment of religion meant, among other things, direct funding of salaries for clergy in the established churches but not in others. Today an "establishment of religion" is grossly urged to be any, often even the most general, public expression of faith and history. By Washington's testimony, we know today's view is obdurately incorrect.

The view that argues for cutting "under God" from the pledge is so extreme it violates common sense. And where do we want our country to go with such a ruling? To join Europe in plunging headfirst into the secular abyss? Let us continue to pledge our allegiance to one nation under God. Or in the words of the Declaration: the Creator, the Lawgiver, the Supreme Judge of the World, and Divine Providence.

An Atheist Addresses the Separation of Church and State

Michael Newdow

Whether the First Amendment intended to bar religion in all public forums is a question that continues to generate great controversy. Many believe that some connections between religious establishments and the government are beneficial—using government funds to support parochial schools or permitting religious displays on government property, for example. Others argue that any religious practice that crosses into the public sphere is anathema to democracy. In the personal account that follows, Michael Newdow describes why he supports this latter view. An atheist activist, Newdow sued his daughter's school district in an attempt to eliminate the phrase "under God" from the Pledge of Allegiance. In 2004 the case went to the Supreme Court, where Newdow argued that the recitation of "under God" in a public school is tantamount to governmental endorsement of religion, which is expressly prohibited by the Constitution. Although the Court ruled that Newdow could not sue on behalf of his daughter, the case fostered widespread public debate about the relationship between government and citizens and the extent of religious liberty in general.

Why did I do it? The answer is easy: our current system is wrong. We have rules, and we're supposed to abide by them, but we haven't been abiding by them at all in the arena of the relationship between government and citizens. We've taken a purely religious ideal—one that millions of Americans expressly deny—and incorporated it into our government. Such activity is expressly prohibited by our Constitution. This is my country just as much as it is anyone else's, and I demand from my government the same respect for my views regarding religion that is given to those with alternative ideals. I'm not someone the majority "tolerates." I don't thank the masses for "allowing" me to not worship as I please. I am not a second-class citizen who should be seen and not heard.

Michael Newdow, "Why I Did It: The 'Under God' and Chaplaincy Plaintiff Speaks Out," *Free Inquiry,* vol. 23, Winter 2003. Copyright © 2003 by the Council for Democratic and Secular Humanism, Inc. Reproduced by permission.

The United States of America is just as much an atheistic entity as it is a theistic entity, with zero being the measure of each. When Congress placed "In God We Trust" on all our coins and currency, when it inserted "under God" into the Pledge of Allegiance, when the Supreme Court starts its sessions with "God save the United States and this honorable court," when presidents take their oaths of office with chaplains offering prayers to God, when every legislative session begins with a prayer to God—and on and on—those who disbelieve in a supreme being are explicitly told that "they are outsiders, not full members of the political community," while theistic Americans are told "that they are insiders, favored members of the political community." That language—repeated time and again by the Supreme Court in describing Establishment Clause violations—details exactly what has been occurring with increasing frequency in our society. The responses of our legislators and our president in the aftermath of the Pledge case decision serve only to highlight the depth of the constitutional transgression.

A Civil Rights Campaign

This is a civil rights campaign, as important and as serious as any in our history. To be sure, other politically disenfranchised minorities—such as women, people of color, and the disabled—have the added burden of physical attributes that make them immediately identifiable. Yet the biases and prejudices each class has endured are little different. Government cannot eliminate invidious opinions, but it can—and, when the opinions are based on religious differences, it constitutionally must—stop fostering such beliefs. We greatly improved our society when we altered our laws to stop encouraging racial segregation, barring women from the workplace, and ignoring the disabled. The goal of the Pledge lawsuit is only to attain further improvement.

In 1958, a Gallup poll revealed that 53 percent of our citizens would not vote for a Black candidate for president merely on the basis of race. In 1999, the last time the poll was taken, the figure was 4 percent. For Catholics, Jews, and women, the latest "would not vote for" figures were 4 percent, 6 percent, and 7 percent, respectively. Yet when it came to atheists, that 1999 poll showed that 48 percent of Americans still would not vote for someone merely on that religious basis. In my opinion, this sort of prejudice is in no small measure perpetuated when our government tells everyone with a coin in his or her pocket that our nation officially, openly—even *proudly*—proclaims that disrespecting atheists is fine.

Could my quest for equality backfire? Absolutely. I have little doubt that the coffers of the pro-God activists have been significantly enriched as a result of the Pledge litigation, and we've already heard calls to place God into our Constitution. Yes, the official antipathy towards atheistic Americans may grow to even greater levels, and even more blatant discrimination may ensue.

But the same possibility of failure was present in the past civil rights campaigns. Thus I'm optimistic and planning on ultimate success. As Americans now opposed to these changes start to appreciate the plight of atheists, I hope they will increase their understanding of religious freedom. As we've seen with *Brown v. Board of Education*, the Nineteenth Amendment, and the Americans with Disabilities Act, when government no longer supports a pervasive personal prejudice, that personal prejudice becomes less pervasive. When our laws recognize that atheists can be role models as positive and strong as Americans of any other life stance, we will further promote the diversity that has so benefited our society. The possibility of an African-American, female, or disabled individual being elected president is no longer remote. The same can be, should be—and, I hope, soon will be—the case for one who is atheistic.

CHAPTER 3

THE RIGHT TO PRIVACY

Contemporary Issues
Companion

THE RIGHT TO PRIVACY IS A MODERN CONCEPT

Amitai Etzioni

In the following viewpoint, legal scholar Amitai Etzioni examines the legal doctrines and court cases that established contemporary notions of privacy. According to Etzioni, society's tendency to view privacy as an inviolable right is a relatively recent phenomenon: Prior to *Roe v. Wade* and other landmark cases of the 1960s and 1970s, for example, concerns for the public welfare overrode many privacy privileges. In contrast, the current trend to excessively protect privacy rights may undermine the common good, particularly in the areas of public health and safety. Etzioni exhorts America to reformulate its conception of privacy to include consideration not only for individual liberties, but also for the needs of society. Amitai Etzioni is a professor at George Washington University and the author of more than thirty books, including *The New Golden Rule: Community and Morality in a Democratic Society* and *The Limits of Privacy*, from which the following is excerpted.

The tendency to allow privacy considerations to take precedence over concerns for public safety and health is not accidental. It reflects fundamental conceptions that are deeply embedded in our civic culture, public policies, and jurisprudence. The evidence presented [here] points to the need for a different conception of privacy, one that accords it equal standing with the common good, without privileging either value.

To reconceptualize privacy, a highly revered right, may seem offensive, almost sacrilegious. We traditionally view individual rights as strong moral claims with universal appeal, indeed we perceive them as inalienable rights. Although we also realize that individual rights were formulated under certain historical conditions, we tend to conceive of these formulations as truths rather than mores fashioned for a given time that are open to amendment as conditions change.

I argue in the following . . . that privacy is a contingent concept. Although some vague notion of privacy exists in most, if not all, societies, the specific way we treat privacy in our law and culture is a recent phenomenon, and one that has already been recast at various times. In other words, privacy is hardly a near-sacred concept that cannot be reformulated.

I also show that the governing formulation of privacy in our society and time treats it as an unbounded good, privileging it over the common good. This conception was well suited to the sociohistorical conditions that prevailed from the formulation of privacy as a legal concept until roughly 1960. However, in the wake of the rise of radical individualism between 1960 and the 1990s, a new conception of privacy is called for, one that does not privilege privacy over the common good but rather is open to balance with concerns for social responsibilities, a communitarian concept.

Privacy Arguments Reexamined

A reexamination of the often-told legal history of privacy in American society helps to illuminate the nature of the arguments used to "extrapolate" privacy as a right from the common law and the Constitution.

In examining the arguments that were used to formulate the legal doctrines that support privacy in American law, I discuss three stages of development: pre-1890 (utilizing principles derived from property rights to protect privacy); 1890 to 1965 (generally considered the era during which a right to privacy was developed, largely as a part of tort law); and post-1965 (a period that has seen a major expansion of the right to privacy, particularly with regard to its constitutional basis). Although my discussion focuses on legal concepts, I cannot stress enough that . . . these concepts have parallels in civic culture and play a major role in the decisions of policymakers.

Before 1890 American society, like many others, had a vague social concept of privacy, albeit one that was not embedded in a distinct legal doctrine or constitutional right. Although there were several legal cases defending some aspect of what later would be called privacy, these typically relied on the well-established right to private property. For example, harming a person's reputation through the revelation of private details was deemed legally redressable because it was thought to do damage to something one owned (i.e., one's reputation), rather than because it was viewed as an invasion of privacy.

The right to private property was, in turn, treated as semisacred: a reflection of a natural law, an inalienable right, and an unmitigated, or at least strongly privileged, good. John Locke, who heavily influenced American thinking on these matters at the time, wrote that property is based in "an original law of nature" that "still takes place" even though societies "have made and multiplied positive laws [laws created by humans] to determine property."

Classical liberals did recognize that the rights of an individual could be asserted only up to the point where such exercise intruded on the liberties of others, and thus individual rights were, in a sense, "limited." But such limitations were not, as a rule, considered for the common good. It was thus typically assumed that property owners were free to do with their property as they deemed fit unless and until their actions plainly impinged on the rights of others. Even then, the burden of proof fell on those who would limit the use of private property, and no principled concessions were recognized to serve socially formulated conceptions of the good.

The Right to Be Let Alone

The next marker in the legal history of privacy is an 1890 essay by Samuel D. Warren and Louis D. Brandeis, which served as the basis for hundreds of legal cases in the century that followed and is considered "the most influential law review article ever published." Warren and Brandeis advanced the novel claim that the right to privacy is conceptually distinct from other freedoms, particularly the right to private property. (As others have observed, the authors were far more explicit in rejecting the notion that privacy is derived from other rights than they were in articulating any specific legal foundation for privacy.)

Warren and Brandeis framed their argument in terms of "the right to be let alone," a right the two assumed to be self-evident. Indeed, Warren and Brandeis referred to the "precincts of private and domestic life"—implying the capability to isolate oneself from public spheres and the community—as "sacred," a term typically employed to designate values or precepts of the highest authority, ones that should not be touched, let alone reined in. (It is indicative of the reverence for rights in general and for privacy in particular that the term "sacred" is frequently employed by people who otherwise draw on no religious images, terminologies, or beliefs.) As invoked, the right to be let alone stands supreme and apart from other considerations; it presumes that all people can be left alone as much as they desire—completely if they so prefer—without restricting other persons' abilities to exercise their own right to be left alone to the fullest extent. Nor is there any apparent recognition that if the members of a community exercise this liberty in full, the common good will be shortchanged.

Later authorities referred to privacy as an "inalienable right," thereby denoting its powerful claim and trump standing. (Trumps are defined as "reasons that can be played against any and all ethical concerns.") Indeed, as Justice [Oliver Wendell] Holmes stated: "Rights tend to declare themselves absolute to their logical extreme." As the right to privacy is viewed as inalienable right, it does not yield to the common good. "Moreover," [legal scholar] William Lund observed, "any citizen who manages to get an interest wrapped in the cloak of a right appears to have an absolute claim against other considerations." [The legal scholar Louis] Henkin has made the communitarian point that "consideration has focused on defining the private right of privacy, with little regard to our other balance, the competing 'public good.'" He added that although this lack of balance characterizes applications of the Bill of Rights generally, the public good has been given particularly short shrift in the area of privacy.

Moreover, there has been a strong tendency to treat privacy either as a cardinal element of autonomy (or liberty), or to treat these concepts as if they were synonymous with privacy, further extending the reverence for privacy. [Harvard law professor] Charles Fried adds that "men feel that invasion of that right injures them in their very humanity," and in regard to respect, love, friendship, and trust, "without privacy they [respect, love, etc.] are simply inconceivable."

Dignity and Decency

Others have claimed that privacy is intimately associated with our most profound values, our understanding of what it means to be an autonomous moral agent capable of self-reflection and choice, and that its violation is "demeaning to individuality [and] an affront to personal dignity," that is, its violation offends the core of Western values. [Legal scholar] Jean Cohen adds that "a constitutionally protected right to personal privacy is indispensable to any modern conception of freedom."

All of these arguments paint a picture of the right to privacy as an unmitigated good, at least as a strongly privileged value. Indeed, few individualists (a term used here to refer to civil libertarians, libertarians, classical liberals, and contemporary classical liberals) even broach the question of whether there can be excessive privacy. Avishai Margalit [professor of philosophy at the Hebrew University in Jerusalem], for instance, simply states that "the institutions of a decent society must not encroach upon personal privacy," recognizing no principled situations in which the common good might require some limitations on privacy. Glen O. Robinson [professor of law at the University of Virginia] points out that, in "controversies over regulating communities and community activities, most legal scholars and judges start with a [classical] liberal bias." This legal approach is particularly well summarized by Stanley I. Benn [author of *Public and Private in Social Life*]:

> The liberal . . . claims not merely a private capacity—an area of action in which he is not responsible to the state for what he does so long as he respects certain minimal rights of others; he claims further that this is the residual category, that the onus is on anyone who claims he is accountable. . . . There is room for a good deal of disagreement about the extent to which considerations like those of general economic well-being, social equality, or national security justify pressing back the frontiers of the private, and thus holding men responsible for the way they conduct their daily business. For the liberal, however, every step he is forced to take in that direction

counts as retreat from a desirable state of affairs, one in which, because men may please themselves, what they are about is properly no one's business but their own.

Landmark Cases

The third stage of the development of the legal foundations of privacy is commonly recognized as commencing with cases such as *Griswold v. Connecticut* (1965), *Eisenstadt v. Baird* (1972), and *Roe v. Wade* (1973), all of which deal with reproductive choices. Using the early 1960s as a baseline, the period before the cases that lay the foundations of a constitutional right to privacy were decided, one sees that the prevailing conceptions of the common good were very strongly privileged and left relatively little room for considerations of privacy and autonomy. Thus, the use, distribution, and sale of contraceptives was outlawed even for married couples. Abortion was banned by law in most states; it was allowed only to save the life of the mother.

Following these landmark court decisions of the 1960s and 1970s, the situation changed drastically. To a large extent, age-old prohibitions that had been imposed in the name of what was considered the common good were struck down. A new constitutional conception of privacy, a right that is not so much as mentioned in the Constitution, was generated—and privileged.

Griswold, the first of these reproductive choice cases, is commonly credited with establishing a general constitutional right to privacy. In that case, the Supreme Court ruled that a Connecticut statute forbidding the use of contraceptives violated the right of marital privacy. Thus, overnight, behavior that had been banned (as far as the law was concerned) was transformed into one that married couples could engage in without limitations. Privacy was now honored. (To note that no limitations were set on this new right is not to suggest that they should have been set, but rather to highlight the dramatic nature of the reversal of the previous position.)

This new right was soon extended. In *Eisenstadt*, the Court went further and invalidated a ban on the *distribution* of contraceptives, even to unmarried couples. In a subsequent case, *Carey v. Population Services International* (1977), limitations on the sale of contraceptives to minors were removed. In these cases, too, the Court did not introduce or explicitly acknowledge any qualifications or limitations on the liberty in question. Protection for privacy had become almost absolute. As Louis Henkin observes, "The Court paid virtually no attention to the State's possible purpose or motive in outlawing contraception." And although *Griswold* was limited to the use of contraceptives by married couples, *Eisenstadt* created a new, much broader conception of privacy, that of the individual: A person could carry this right anywhere; it was a freedom that would no longer be confined to one's bedroom or house.

To reiterate, I am *not* suggesting that the various prohibitions on the use and sale of contraceptives or on abortion should have been allowed to stand. My argument only points to the unbounded nature of the position embraced. No limits on the right to privacy in the name of some other consideration—for instance, respect for community values or special considerations for parents' responsibilities for minors—were allowed to stand.

In *Roe v. Wade*, the Court further expanded the right of privacy by striking down bans on abortion. This case, however, was arguably somewhat less comprehensive than the others. Although the Court did not let stand any limitations on terminating pregnancies, it explicitly stated that it rejected the unbounded approach and formulated some criteria under which states could ban abortion. Justice Harry Blackmun wrote:

> Some amici argue that the woman's right is absolute and she is entitled to terminate her pregnancy at whatever time, in whatever way, and for whatever reason she alone chooses. With this we do not agree. . . . A state may properly assert important interests in safeguarding health, in maintaining medical standards, and in protecting potential life.

The Court ruled that the states may override a woman's decision "whether or not to terminate her pregnancy" if the state's interest is "compelling." And the Court, by introducing distinctions between the trimesters of pregnancy, indirectly legitimated more regulation of the third trimester than of the second, and more of the second than of the first.

One may side with those who believe the Court should have allowed the bans on abortion to stand or with those who hold that the ruling was too restrictive; neither position alters the observation here about the basic nature of the argument at issue: *Roe v. Wade* is an important case in which a behavior that had previously been controlled by the state was freed to be subject to personal choice.

In short, the approach to privacy that evolved, first in tort law and then in Supreme Court decisions concerning reproductive choice cases, treats privacy as an unbounded good. In its more moderate form, this approach lays the burden of proof on those who seek consideration for other claims, thus treating the common good at best as secondary.

Historical Context for the Privileging of Privacy

The nature of these individualist arguments is best understood in the historical context in which they arose. The extrapolation of a legal right to privacy from common law cases, from newly fashioned arguments, and ultimately from the Constitution took place late in the long development of legal individual rights, a process that was itself an indication of the growing value accorded to individual dignity and liberty. Indeed, one can read the writings of John Locke, Adam Smith, and some of those of John Stuart Mill as arguments for individual rights and liberty that were formulated in authoritarian and excessively communal historical periods and as arguments for rolling back extensive and oppressive societal controls imposed by both the state and the community. Not surprisingly, social philosophers whose societies experienced these highly restrictive conditions did not concern themselves with the danger of legitimizing individual rights to excess—no more than one is concerned about overusing a town's water supply in the depths of the rainy season after decades of more than ample rainfall, indeed flooding.

Historically, the formulation of privacy is a late addition to the long list of rights. Its development took place several generations after the first recognition in American law of the rights to free speech, freedom of association, and freedom of worship, among others. In fact, Warren and Brandeis are explicit about this point in their 1890 article. They open their renowned essay with a discussion of their belief that it was time for the common law to "grow to meet the demands of society," much as it had done on previous occasions when social circumstances had shifted. The same approach is reflected in the work of T.H. Marshall, who viewed Western history as a relentless march toward increasingly expansive spheres of rights, growing from legal to political to socioeconomic rights, with little concern or suggestion that rights might be overextended or intrude on other common goods.

American Culture Paradoxically Values Privacy, Exhibitionism, and Surveillance

Wendy Kaminer

In the following selection, Wendy Kaminer examines what she calls an American paradox: The same populace that professes a deep regard for personal privacy has simultaneously produced a culture rife with voyeurism and exhibitionism, as evidenced by the popularity of reality-based programming and tabloid television, for example, or the willingness of many to tolerate governmental surveillance. Kaminer asserts that although many people routinely forfeit their privacy, they do so with the knowledge that they also have the right to function as private individuals if they choose. Kaminer concludes that this fundamental personal liberty—the right to choose what to reveal or conceal—is essential to civil society and must be vigorously upheld. Kaminer is a senior correspondent for the *American Prospect*, a contributing editor at the *Atlantic Monthly*, and the author of several books, including *Free for All: Defending Liberty in America Today*, from which the following is excerpted.

American culture thrives on contradictions. It exalts individualism and is rife with the conformity so essential to consumerism. It preaches self-reliance and personal accountability while enriching pop therapists who provide reassurances and excuses to the anxious middle class. It nurtures feminism and encourages face-lifts.

So in late-twentieth-century America, we should not have been entirely surprised by the paradoxical convergence of an exhibitionist, voyeuristic culture and a growing demand for law enforcement surveillance with pervasive concern about privacy. By 2000, the intensity of these opposing trends was particularly dramatic. While "reality TV" shows debuted and security cameras in public places proliferated, Democratic and Republican pollsters were attesting to a "groundswell" of concern about privacy, which politicians rushed to address.

During the 2000 campaign, George Bush declared himself a "privacy rights person." Al Gore speechified about privacy on the Internet. Congress considered hundreds of privacy protection bills.

Privacy became a familiar, pervasive concern in the 1990s, as technology and the continued expansion of the prosecutorial state threatened our ability to keep secrets. Raising the alarm about government or private industry invading our personal lives, civil libertarians tended to assume that practically everyone valued privacy. According to a 1995 Harris Poll, 82 percent of respondents were concerned about personal privacy (compared to 64 percent in 1978).

Willing to Trade Away Privacy

But we routinely traded privacy for the promise of security, welcoming cameras that monitored parking garages, elevators, or banks and meekly tolerating the senseless demands of airlines for easily falsified photo IDs. After September 11, we quickly became accustomed to exhibiting IDs to office-building security guards—who would have admitted Osama Bin Laden if he shaved his beard, changed his clothes, and showed them a picture ID. Fear of crime or terrorism and the comfort of illusory security measures usually prevails over privacy.

With equal enthusiasm, we traded privacy for fame, or the hope of it. If notoriety is a threat, sometimes it is also a promise. Americans have long been attracted and revolted by exposure, at least since Louis Brandeis and Samuel Warren published their landmark treatise on privacy in the *Harvard Law Review* over a century ago. Today, with the digital revolution making privacy as obsolete as the rotary phone, it's worth stressing that their nineteenth-century plea for the right to be let alone was inspired by new technology, mainly photography. Brandeis and Warren were concerned with the "unauthorized circulation of portraits of private persons" in the press and with the rise of gossip. They wanted to create a remedy for involuntary, "unwarranted" invasions of privacy. (They recognized that privacy rights should not always protect public figures engaged in matters of public interest, recognizing as well the difficulties of distinguishing between public and private concerns.)

A Culture Obsessed with Gossip and Exhibitionism

Brandeis and Warren treasured privacy as essential to human dignity, and they lived at a time when exhibitionism was not respectable, much less a sign of mental health. It would have been hard for them to imagine that dignity would one day seem a small price to pay for a moment of fame. "The general object in view is to protect the privacy of private life," they wrote. What happens when private life loses allure, when, like trees falling in the forest, people want someone watching to make sure they exist? Gossip becomes a preeminent form of information. Over one hundred years ago, Brandeis and Warren worried that gossip was no longer an idle pastime. It was becoming "a trade," they warned, presciently describing the dangers it posed: Gossip appeals to our baser instincts, the "weak side of human nature" that takes pleasure in the "misfortunes and frailties" of others. It was dignified by print and "crowds space available" for discussion of public issues. The trouble with gossip, they eloquently observed, was that "it usurps the place of interest in brains capable of other things."

We surely saw proof of that during the 1990s, with the rise of tabloid TV. As many critics have noted, we were collectively obsessed with trivialities, which generally involved the details of other people's private lives. There was some self-consciousness about the elevation of gossip to news: Pundits were forever telling us why someone's private conduct qualified as a public issue. But the explanations were perfunctory; everyone knew that gossip was news, regardless.

By the time the scandals of the 1990s broke, we already inhabited a talk-show culture that provided forums for the exhibitionists among us and entertainment for the voyeurs. It was spawned by popular therapies that taught us to fear repression or denial more than exposure. The therapeutic culture pathologized privacy, silence, and stoicism and promoted the belief that healthy people talk about themselves—sometimes incessantly and often in public—at least in support groups. Discretion about your private life was often facilely equated with repression.

Late-twentieth-century liberation movements, notably feminism and the gay rights movement, contributed to conflicts and confusion over privacy. In the gay community, where discretion had been forced upon people (where it could fairly be called repressive) exposure became a political act, not simply a therapeutic one. Unfortunately, it also became a controversial political mandate, as a few closeted homosexuals were outed. Some people who once had secrecy forced upon them felt entitled to force exposure on others. Feminists also fought simultaneously for privacy and publicity. They defended personal and familial privacy when it protected reproductive rights and condemned privacy when it protected men who abused their wives and children, or merely enjoyed pornography.

Granting Government Invasive Powers

So in the mid-1990s, a report that over 80 percent of Americans were concerned with privacy didn't tell us very much. Did over 80 percent of Americans believe that police shouldn't have the power to take DNA samples from suspected criminals or that sex offenders shouldn't be identified to their neighbors? Did they want to limit the power of police to conduct warrantless searches? In recent years, the courts expanded it, with no outcry from the public. Long before September 11, people gave government broad powers to wiretap. They supported a war on drugs that eviscerated the Fourth Amendment and the privacy rights it was intended to protect. Did 80 percent of all Americans believe that welfare recipients have privacy rights against social workers or that employers have no right to demand drug tests of employees? Would over 80 percent of all Americans have turned down the chance to appear on the *Today Show* or *Oprah*? How many Americans were ready to throw out their credit cards?

It has always been difficult to talk about privacy in general. On September 10, 2001, you would not have found majority support for the privacy rights of criminal suspects or welfare recipients. You would have found considerable public support for maintaining the privacy of medical records, except perhaps when the government claims a need to investigate Medicaid fraud—someone else's fraud, of course. People tend to regard privacy the way they regard other civil liberties or tax breaks: they support the ones they use.

Civil libertarians often say that you shouldn't support any new restriction on liberty unless you're willing to be subjected to it. But many people take the opposite approach, supporting repressive laws and policies that they expect will only be applied to others—criminals, terrorists, or recent immigrants. Shortly after September 11, one man identified as a libertarian told the *New York Times* that he understood the need for racial profiling, so long as it wasn't used against "ordinary people." Of course, ordinary people constitute profiling's primary victims. If law enforcement agents were psychic and could intuit the presence of terrorists and other criminals, they'd have no need for profiling.

Under Constant Watch

The value of surveillance to a fearful, insecure, and intrusive society is its ubiquity. Governmental and corporate authorities cast their surveillance nets over all of us, hoping to deter high crimes and low misdemeanors (like shopping on the Internet at work) and promising to snare only the guilty few. How do you escape surveillance? Maintaining privacy has long required the constant vigilance of ordinary people—vigilance that few of us have exercised. For years, people gave up their privacy inadvertently, as they gave up their social security numbers to department store clerks in order to establish charge accounts. People claimed they cared about privacy, but God forbid they didn't have a Macy's charge card.

Sometimes people were simply unaware of the threats to their privacy. A 1998 survey by the New York Civil Liberties Union found at least 2,380 surveillance cameras monitoring public spaces; an estimated 2,000 of them were private. Sometimes people had little choice but to forfeit their privacy rights. Millions of employees have been monitored in the workplace: Employers read their E-mails, monitor their computer use, and review personal computer files, or they demand drug tests.

But while many people resent being spied upon, some have begun to feel entitled to spy upon others: New computer programs allow people to monitor their spouse's E-mails or on-line reading habits. Cameras in day-care centers allow parents to keep children, and day-care workers, under constant watch. Armed with video cameras, people tape their children incessantly; the middle class has probably reared a generation of performers. It's not surprising when young denizens of the cyber-culture install cameras in their own homes and exhibit themselves 24/7 on the Net.

Of course, many of their parents didn't exactly shy away from exhibiting themselves. Before the pop therapies of the 1980s encouraged people to spill the toxic secrets of family life, the baby boom generation was supposedly letting it all hang out. The counterculture was always self-consciously attention grabbing. It was trumped by talk shows, which, in turn, were trumped by reality programming, which, oddly enough, came into prominence at about the same time that polls were showing strong public concern about protecting privacy. While media stories on protecting privacy abounded, media encroachments on privacy astounded. Over 20 million people tuned in to watch *Survivor*, which was soon followed by *Big Brother*, the show that confined ten strangers to a house for one hundred days and subjected them to constant surveillance. Soon, reality-based shows were commonplace. Reporters polled experts to find out what this phenomenon said about our psyche. If you didn't watch reality TV, you could always read about it—while you worried about your anonymity if you were reading on-line. The press loved the story of reality TV but covered the privacy debate as well, mirroring the culture's cognitive dissonance.

Celebrity

But the contradictions in our relationship to privacy are not all that difficult to resolve: People exhibit in the belief that they can choose what to reveal and what to conceal. Even exhibitionists have many things to hide. Think of [former president] Bill Clinton. Exhibitionists plan on exposing only what they choose to expose. They exhibit in the belief that they're in control of their public presentation. But their control is most tenuous. Think again of Clinton. Even the president can't control a hostile or prurient press.

Once you enter the public sphere, you put yourself at the mercy of public curiosity and its handmaiden—the media. That's why celebrities have press agents. That's why people who have actively sought celebrity—rock stars, models, or movie stars—find themselves in the anomalous position of demanding privacy. Nicole Kidman once appeared half nude on the cover of *Newsweek* next to a tag line promising she would discuss her marriage to Tom Cruise and their fight for privacy. Only in a culture that values secrecy but craves celebrity could you make a straight-faced plea for privacy by posing barely clothed on the cover of a national news magazine and talking about your marriage with millions of strangers. When [reclusive author] J.D. Salinger says he values his privacy I believe him. Nicole Kidman's desire for privacy is apparently a bit more equivocal.

But Kidman's appearance on *Newsweek*'s cover only proved the point: People who voluntarily surrender their privacy may not want it wrested from them. It's not privacy that people value so much as the power to control what is revealed and concealed. We want both public and private lives, and we want the power to police the boundaries between them. But in a surveillance state, that power is surrendered by individuals and wielded by the government.

Parental Government

In a democracy, the creation of a surveillance state has to be predicated on consent, and consent is obtained by popularizing an avuncular image of a government that monitors us benignly. In Great Britain, surveillance cameras routinely monitor public spaces, with relatively little opposition. Privacy expert Jeffrey Rosen has observed (in the *New York Times Magazine*) that the British public tends to regard its intrusive government not as a Big Brother but as a kindly uncle or aunt.

Paternalistic government inevitably gains popularity during crises, when people need to view the president as a father figure. The day after Bush's address to Congress on September 20, 2001, one self-identified Democrat interviewed on National Public Radio referred to the president approvingly as our "daddy in chief." This suggests that we're a nation of children, and children are used to being monitored by their parents; in fact, they take comfort in it. Having Mommy and Daddy watching, even from a distance, makes children feel safe. People feel threatened or at least unsettled by surveillance when an apparently hostile or indifferent authority conducts it. They find surveillance comforting when they believe it's offered in a spirit of loving protectiveness. So, the more politicians and law enforcement agents scare us about crime or terrorism, the more we need to trust in their good faith and abilities; the more we trust them, the more we welcome or at least accept surveillance.

The craving for community, as well as security, can also undermine privacy. There are some crude, obvious ways in which communal life and codes of behavior threaten individual liberty. One conservative pundit has opined that less privacy would probably lead to more virtue. We would have less adultery, he suggested, if people monitored each other's private lives. Evidence of this assertion is scarce; the public has been monitoring the private lives of celebrities for some years without discouraging any of them from fooling around. In any case, my own vision of a virtuous society is not one that's built on a network of neighborhood spies.

But even the most benevolent communities pose subtle threats to privacy. Religion has always been an obvious and important source of community. (Even atheists or agnostics sometimes go to church for the sake of their social lives.) But the more we focus on religion as a public function, the less respect we may have for it as a private prerogative.

This was evident in the 2000 presidential campaign, when former senator Bill Bradley refused to answer questions about his religious beliefs, asserting that religion was a private matter and not appropriate fodder for a political campaign. That was, or should have been, an unremarkable observation; yet it garnered attention because other candidates were flaunting their religiosity, the way they flaunted their happy marriages. A desire not to talk publicly about a personal belief in God was considered suspicious or, at least, noteworthy; respect for religious privacy had surely declined.

Or, consider the role of public religious rituals and displays when people came together to mourn the September 11 attack. It engendered an understandable urge to pray and grieve collectively, which partly reflected the sense that the nation had suffered a collective blow. But when communities in crisis exaggerate and exalt religion's public function, public life can expand at the expense of the private realm. The ideology of mourning that prevailed immediately after September 11 reflected the influence of pop therapies as well as religion. A familiar therapeutic ethic prevailed: Exhibitionism was encouraged. (Remember the Cantor Fitzgerald executive who cried to Larry King?) Stoicism and self-containment were suspect.

Anonymity

What defenses do we have against communal, cultural, or governmental incursions on our privacy? Perhaps technology can help us subvert surveillance, as well as establish it. Perhaps America's libertarian streak (evident in the digital culture) will encourage the individualism that evaluates cultural and communal norms instead of simply obeying them. But the best defense of privacy may be anonymity. People can best tolerate surveillance that doesn't threaten anonymity—and plays no role in monitoring virtue. New Yorkers in high-rise apartments have long felt free to spy on each other, so long as both watcher and watchee remained anonymous. I frequent a nude beach in the summer; I'm perfectly comfortable there, so long as I don't encounter anyone I know.

It is, therefore, important to distinguish privacy from anonymity. The more anonymous you feel, the less privacy you need. Consider the plight of homeless people. They have virtually no privacy living on the street, but they also have no public identities. They're practically invisible to many of us. The curse of their anonymity perversely affords them a modicum of privacy. The more uncomfortable you make people, the more invisible you may become. But social neglect is a high price to pay for anonymity.

And anonymity is a high price to pay for privacy. I'm happy on the nude beach not encountering friends or colleagues, but off the beach, I'd be lost without them. What's the lesson of this? What do we lose when we lose control of privacy and must resort to anonymity? We lose both liberty—the freedom to be ourselves in public—and the ability to form community. And if we can't form community, we can't act collectively, or politically. The loss of privacy could deter the formation of political movements—including movements against surveillance. It's not just that surveillance will chill dissent—as it is intended to do. It's that our willingness to gather together and act collectively may be predicated on the confidence that we can still exist and thrive as private individuals.

Secrecy is essential to civil society and social relations. Some applaud the "openness" (or shamelessness) of the new exhibitionism, in the belief that it will bring us together. But social life would be intolerable for many of us without the possibility of solitude. Without it, community, as well as individualism, is at risk. The more public space expands, the more it threatens public life. We need not know everything about each other, so that we don't have to feel exposed by every encounter. Privacy makes public life possible.

Technology Is a Threat to Privacy

Eric J. Gertler

Privacy is under siege, according to Eric J. Gertler, author of Prying Eyes: Protect Your Privacy from People Who Sell to You, Snoop on You, and Steal from You. In the following excerpt, Gertler details the myriad ways that modern technology imperils personal privacy. With the advent of powerful electronic networks, for example, vast amounts of personal information are routinely monitored, stored, and shared in cyberspace—online shopping habits, medical records, and many other private affairs. At the same time, Gertler writes, the terrorist attacks on September 11, 2001, dramatically altered the way Americans view privacy: Faced with the threat of terror, the public's desire to achieve greater national security often trumps concerns for privacy and other civil liberties.

Today's most pressing [privacy] concerns involve new challenges to individual privacy resulting from technology—the same issue that [Louis] Brandeis and [Samuel] Warren wrote about in 1890, following the invention of instant photographs and tabloids, that "what is whispered in the closet shall be proclaimed from the housetops." The same desire to preserve "the sacred precincts of private and domestic life" applies today.

The Internet and other new technologies, such as camera cell phones and other wireless devices are exciting and important developments but are still in their early stages, so the full scope of their threat and risks has not been fully explored. Many of these technologies have already led to an increase in crime, including the creation of computer viruses, the destruction and theft of sensitive personal information, Internet cyberstalkers, credit card theft, identity theft, and much more.

If you're like some people, you may not really care about privacy until you lose it. For example, you probably don't think about unwanted privacy invasions until that telemarketing call wakes you up or interrupts your dinner, or until identity theft or credit card fraud depletes your bank account, demolishes your credit, and creates havoc in your life.

Uses of Private Information

What you may not realize is that the ways in which your sensitive personal information may be used against you are unlimited. For example, you may innocently share personal information in an online user group whose members are HIV-positive, or you might buy illicit items and later discover that information about your purchases has been entered in a database and combined with other personal information about you. When the database is purchased or shared, it is possible that you could be hurt if, say, an employer, insurance company, spouse, or others see the sensitive information that you don't want disclosed.

Notwithstanding these risks to you, governments and businesses gather and rely on your personal information for a variety of important reasons. The government may use it to test the effectiveness of new medical drugs, for example. Courts use personal information to track down deadbeat dads who fail to pay their child obligations. Law enforcement agencies use it to track down criminals. People in need of organ and blood donations or bone marrow transfers depend on accurate and up-to-date databanks on donors.

Businesses use personal information to better understand their markets so they may develop new products, improve customer service, or even develop personalized services that consumers demand. Over the long term, the collection of such data may lead to more effective marketing and theoretically helps reduce the consumer price for goods.

Nevertheless, networked commercial databases that maintain personal information about you are a growing threat to your privacy. Today, nearly every company that markets consumer products is compiling databases to track and monitor its customer base. In addition, although estimates vary, privacy experts believe hundreds if not thousands of data aggregators are in the business of maintaining comprehensive information about you. Companies use these lists to solicit consumers with special promotions or offers. For example, Acxiom, a database company based in Arkansas, has developed and maintains a real-time database that collects and processes information on nearly every American household. The company's clients can use the comprehensive information stored in its database to develop and deepen relationships with customers based on all sorts of criteria, including zip code, income, lifestyle, or even a profile of "timeless elders" or "Single City Struggles." Companies will often buy lists from data aggregators and combine these lists with their own customer databases.

The information that many companies track and maintain goes far beyond simple demographic data, such as your name, how much you make, and where you live. Indeed, the extent of available information is limited only by technology itself. Each individual electronic transaction you make—from the use of a credit, debit, or ATM card to "loyalty" cards, online bill payment, and check payment—provides clues to parts of your life. When these individual pieces of information are integrated, they create a vivid picture of you and your personal life. For example, when a supermarket clerk swipes your loyalty card through a scanner, a database links your identity with the bar code on every item you have purchased. Although you may not consider your taste for frozen pizza dinners an especially tantalizing piece of information, when combined with your age, credit standing, ethnicity, religion, and marital status, such information becomes quite interesting to marketers.

The number of companies that offer personalized marketing is growing. The technology these companies use is increasingly efficient, enabling businesses to sort and categorize data to target specific people for specialized marketing purposes. For example, a class-action lawsuit against Metromail Corporation revealed the types of information contained in its database. The computer file on one individual, Beverly Dennis, included nine hundred personal details printed out on twenty-five pages and dating back an entire decade. Among other things, Metromail knew Dennis's income, hobbies, and ailments, her preferred brand of antacid tablets, whether she had dentures, and how often she used room deodorizers, sleeping aids, and hemorrhoid remedies. Another company, the New York–based firm American Student Lists, sells the personal information it gathers on millions of high school students from such diverse sources as driver's licenses, student directories, magazine subscriptions, yearbook publishers, class ring vendors, formal wear companies, fast food companies, and book clubs. There are also companies that sell lists of people with particular medical conditions, ranging from patients who are clinically depressed, women who have yeast infections, and diabetics, to people who suffer from Alzheimer's disease, birth defects, Parkinson's disease, or physical handicaps. The extent to which businesses engage in the trade of personal information is astounding.

September 11 and Your Privacy

Any discussion of privacy rights must be put into the context of the devastating effects of the September 11 terrorist attacks and the consequences associated with the attacks. Without question, September 11 was a watershed in terms of its effect on the American public's views of privacy. Principles and laws established by Brandeis and Douglas and others had set a precedent toward more privacy rights, but September 11 had the opposite effect. As a result of the terrorist attacks, national security became Americans' primary concern and invariably trumped concern for individual privacy.

Prior to September 11, privacy was a key issue in the minds of

Americans. One survey conducted in 1999 by the *Wall Street Journal* and NBC indicated that privacy was the issue of *greatest* concern facing Americans at the turn of the 21st century—more important, ironically, than terrorist attacks on American soil, overpopulation, or global warming. In early 2001, Chief Justice William Rehnquist stated, "Technology now permits millions of important and confidential conversations to occur through a vast system of electronic networks. These advances however raise significant privacy concerns. We are placed in the uncomfortable position of not knowing who might have access to our personal and business e-mails, our medical and financial records, or our cordless and cellular telephone conversations."

In the months before September 11, Americans viewed a company's commitment to an individual's privacy as essential for doing business. In a national survey conducted in September 2000 by the Privacy Council and Privista, survey respondents stated that a company's commitment to privacy was as important as maintaining product satisfaction, offering customer discounts, or having an 800 number for consumer feedback. Moreover, companies that failed—whether intentionally or not—to respect or manage privacy concerns had to deal with the serious consequences of real or perceived privacy violations. For example, after a hostile public reaction, DoubleClick, a successful Internet and technology company, abandoned its plans to integrate its online database of customer profiles with the offline database it had secured when it acquired the company Abacus. Another company, Geocities, now part of Yahoo, was the subject of a privacy violation complaint by the Federal Trade Commission for sharing customer information in a manner inconsistent with its privacy policy. As a result, the company experienced a serious drop in its stock price, though the stock later regained much of its value. The bottom line was clear: companies had to take a serious look at their privacy commitment to their customers.

At the same time, numerous privacy laws were being considered in Congress and in the statehouses. The emphasis on the protection of privacy was moving in the direction of creating new legal rights to privacy, and legislators in both the Democratic and Republican parties were working in tandem to pass legislation. In 2000, for example, fifty privacy bills were pending in Congress, dealing with both online and offline privacy concerns. Such initiatives reflected consumer reactions and polls, and thus both the states and Congress wanted to enhance individual privacy rights.

In the aftermath of September 11, consumer, legislative, and public sentiment changed. The overwhelming desire to achieve greater national security trumped all other concerns. From all perspectives, the world had changed overnight, and the [George W.] Bush administration sought and achieved a new means of dealing with the foreign threat of terrorism. In the world's greatest democracy, privacy and the individual rights associated with it were outweighed by an interest in enhanced national security. What followed stoked unwelcome memories of steps the country had taken in earlier times of great national anxiety, such as the quarantine of the Japanese during World War II and the outing of Communist Party members during the 1950s.

The Patriot Act

Forty-five days after the terrorist attacks of September 11, with little debate or scrutiny in Congress, the government passed the Uniting and Strengthening America by Providing Appropriate Tools Required to Intercept and Obstruct Terrorism Act, more commonly known as the USA Patriot Act or the Patriot Act. The name of the act itself seems to characterize even mild criticism of the act's provisions as unpatriotic—implying that if you're against the Patriot Act, you're unpatriotic. The act considerably expanded the investigative powers of the government and turned two hundred years of jurisprudence on its head. Under the act, the government no longer needs to abide by the standards of "probable cause" required for a search warrant. Rather, law enforcement agents only need to certify that the information they are seeking is relevant to an ongoing criminal investigation. Accordingly, law enforcement agents can broadly access any information relevant to their investigation, including information regarding your personal financial information, your medical records, and your school and library records. You name it, and they can obtain it. More importantly, you may never even know you are being investigated, because law enforcement officials are no longer required to tell you.

In addition to the Patriot Act, the government also sought to develop what it called a Total Information Awareness program. This program would have empowered the government to create a massive database to track all your personal information. With this centralized database, the government would have had the ability to comb through your bank records, tax filings, driver's license information, your credit card purchases, your magazine subscriptions, your online activities, your medical prescriptions, your educational records, and much more. Public outcry ultimately shut down this program in 2003. Despite the demise of the Total Information Awareness program, the government continues to use Carnivore, a computer system developed by the FBI that, when connected to the network of an Internet Service Provider (ISP), can intercept millions of e-mail messages per second. The system monitors the e-mails of both its target and innocent people who use the same ISP. The genie is out of the bottle now that the technology and database capabilities are able to track electronic correspondence.

When the Patriot Act was passed, citizens did not seem upset about the act's provisions, and Congress, the state legislatures, and the courts seemed to agree. Throughout the country, previous legislative initiatives in support of privacy rights were put on the back burner. In keeping with this spirit, in 2002, the United States Foreign Intelligence Surveillance Court of Review issued its first-ever ruling in twenty-five years of existence in which it expanded the government's right to use wiretap surveillance in criminal investigations.

Backlash

As time has passed and the country has moved further from the horrible events of September 11, the public again has demanded legislation that will protect the privacy of citizens from intrusions of both government and business. Beginning in 2003, a number of important legislative actions have taken place in addition to the shutdown of the Total Information Awareness program. For example, on January 1, 2004, the Fair and Accurate Credit Transaction Act of 2003 went into effect helping to protect you against identity theft. The act requires credit bureaus to provide you with one free credit report per year, requires merchants and lenders to provide you with early notification of missed payments, and requires merchants to truncate your credit card number on receipts to the last five digits, among other things. . . . In 2003, the Do Not Call Registry, a federal program that restricts commercial telemarketers from calling you after you register, went into effect. The registry was designed to reduce unwanted phone calls to consumers, especially during the dinner hour. As expected, the response was overwhelmingly positive: more than 7 million telephone numbers were registered on the program's first day; more than 56 million numbers were registered by January 2004. . . . In addition, on January 1, 2004, a federal Internet anti-spamming bill called the Can-Spam Act went into effect, restricting commercial e-mail companies or spammers from using false identities and misleading subject lines. . . . In addition, about 250 municipalities around the country have passed legislation supporting individual rights in direct contravention of the Patriot Act. In December 2003, two federal appeals courts rejected the Bush administration's policy with respect to captives suspected of being terrorists. A New York federal appeals court ruled that the Bush administration lacked authority to detain indefinitely a U.S. citizen arrested in the United States simply by declaring the citizen "an enemy combatant"; and a San Francisco appeals court ruled that it was unconstitutional to imprison noncitizens captured in the Afghan War in Guantanamo Bay, Cuba, without access to an attorney.

THE CRUSADE TO PROTECT PRIVACY IS MISGUIDED

Michael Lind

Michael Lind is the coauthor of *The Radical Center: The Future of American Politics* and a fellow at the New American Foundation, a public policy institute. In the following viewpoint, Lind writes that the privacy debate is being driven by the misguided notion that all privacy losses represent an infringement on personal liberty. In truth, Lind writes, many privacy concerns are insubstantial. Privacy, moreover, is a nebulous concept: There are so many disparate facets to the privacy debate that even situations that merit legitimate concern should not be analyzed as a single "privacy issue," but rather considered individually.

In a remarkable short period of time, "privacy" has moved from the margins to the center of political debate in the United States, Canada and Europe. The nebulous concept today embraces a number of issues, ranging from the serious—the possible abuse of the results of genetic testing by corporations and the government—to the trivial—the sharing of information about consumer preferences among businesses that bombard hapless consumers with unsolicited catalogs and e-mail advertisements. What unites these diverse concerns, according to the emerging consensus, is the danger that new technologies of surveillance, data-recording and data exchange will be put to nefarious purposes. Big Brother, we are cautioned again and again, is finally here—not in the form of a totalitarian state, but of something subtler and perhaps more sinister, a universal surveillance society.

A few thinkers have challenged this perception, among them the communitarian sociologist Amitai Etzioni, who stresses the need to balance individual privacy against the legitimate interests of the community, and the scientist David Brin, who argues that we must adapt to "the transparent society" rather than attempt to prevent its evolution. Despite these dissenters, fear of the imminent erosion of a historic right and of a threatening new, soft totalitarianism, is rapidly becoming the conventional wisdom. It strikes me as not only nonsense,

Michael Lind, "Solving the Privacy Puzzle," *New Leader,* vol. LXXXV, January/February 2002, pp. 15–17.

but dangerous nonsense that could do enormous harm to a great many people.

A Naïve View

The idea that there was a golden age of personal privacy in the past is naïve. Until a few generations ago, most Americans lived on farms or in small towns or crowded neighborhoods where personal privacy, in the contemporary sense, was virtually nonexistent. This was as true of the aristocrat, surrounded most of the time by servants, as it was of the peasant sharing a one- or two-room hut with family and, sometimes, livestock. In a letter of paternal advice to his son, the 19th-century American architect Henry Hobson Richardson warned that confidences should never be committed to paper, because servants were fond of reading letters. The young [novelist] William Faulkner, during a stint as a postmaster, is alleged to have amused himself by reading the mail of his neighbors.

In the era of the telephone party line, operators were notorious for eavesdropping. A woman who worked for the phone company in the 1940s, when operators on roller skates monitored wall-sized batteries of phone wires, once told me that if an operator picked up a particularly salacious conversation, she would motion to her coworkers and they would roll over to listen. As recently as the John F. Kennedy, Lyndon B. Johnson and Richard M. Nixon administrations, the FBI seems to have been wiretapping anyone of any prominence in the United States.

Searching for a constitutional pedigree for their campaign, privacy crusaders in the United States have merely been able to come up with a few tidbits—a quote from Justice Louis D. Brandeis here, an early 20th-century court case about publishing photographs without permission there. The truth is that the notion of privacy in its current elastic sense dates back only to the 1960s and '70s, when it first entered public discourse in connection with reproductive choice in Supreme Court decisions like *Griswold v. Connecticut* (1965) and *Roe v. Wade* (1973). Agglomerating a growing number of distinct controversies and filing all of them under "privacy" is an even later political phenomenon.

There Is No Single Privacy Issue

It is also the simple and misleading modus operandi of the new privacy theorists: They link together discrete disputes that would best be analyzed separately—for instance, the argument about using biometric cameras to catch criminals, and the question of mandatory HIV testing of newborns. Instead of dealing with each case on its own merits, they retreat to the higher, abstract principle of privacy.

To accept the lumping together of different topics as "aspects" of a single "privacy issue" is to engage in the debate on their terms. Worse, it is to put oneself in the unpopular position of being "against" privacy. The sensible alternative would not only be to treat each situation individually, but to recognize personal privacy as just one of several competing factors deserving consideration. This would make it possible to conclude, for example, that corporations should not be allowed to subpoena the PCs of employees to learn whether they are involved in union activity, and that all newborns should be tested for HIV—or the opposite.

An Emotional Crusade

Of course, mine is a minority opinion. The claim that a historic right is on the block, putting our democratic society in jeopardy, is ascendant. But if, as I believe, the conventional wisdom about privacy is deeply confused, what explains its appeal to so many otherwise thoughtful people?

The answer, I would suggest, has less to do with politics than sociology. No one who follows the privacy debate with a degree of objectivity can fail to be impressed by two things: Its tone is peculiarly emotional, and its social base is peculiarly elitist. The emotionalism is familiar from past "moral panics," such as the fear of fluoridation or the much-hyped "epidemics" of child-stealing in the 1980s and church-burning in the 1990s, which turned out later to be fabricated from misunderstood data. The fear that the convergence of high technology with law enforcement and business practices is about to rob us of our privacy has all the hallmarks of a classic, irrational moral panic.

This is especially clear where privacy questions intersect with those involving sex and children. In addition, one is struck by a difference in the reactions of men and women (these are my impressions, but I trust that the experience of others bears them out as well). If advances in camera and computer technology are contributing to the salience of the privacy issue in politics, my sense is that—to put it crudely—women tend to be more obsessed with cameras and men with computers. Women express a disproportionate concern about being objects of male voyeurism. In public discussions of privacy, one hears them repeatedly raise the specter of employers secreting a camera in the women's bathroom. Many of the same women who dread high-tech Peeping Toms, though, appear to be the purchasers of "kindercams" and "nannycams"—the tiny cameras hidden in clocks and other appliances to spy on children and their caretakers.

Men, to judge by their contributions to public discussions of privacy, are less worried about cameras in the bathroom than they are about the boss or the government tracking their surfing on the Web. Furthermore—to make another generalization I believe can be confirmed—this male anxiety is most intense among affluent, college-educated, heterosexuals.

The new privacy crusaders claim they are defending us all against abuses of power by authority. But the groups most likely to suffer from discrimination and exploitation—the working class and poor, members of racial minorities, gays and lesbians—appear to be much less preoccupied with the alleged problem than more mainstream members of the suburban, educated overclass.

The paradox is glaring. The very people who, thanks to their privileged backgrounds, are most likely to be corporate executives and high-level civil servants, tend to be most alarmed about the prospect of corporations and governments being able to acquire information they want to conceal. I have been in rooms full of well-heeled individuals where only one person dissented from the consensus that citizens should be allowed to hide any information they choose from law enforcement agencies by means of encryption devices of the sort used by spies, terrorist organizations and organized crime. I suspect that in a room full of blue-collar workers, a consensus in favor of the law enforcement agencies would be equally pronounced.

Something to Hide

There are two possible explanations. One is that the elite—in particular, elite men—know from personal experience how abusive business and government can be, and rationally fear giving employers and government agencies high-tech tools to gather, codify and transmit information. The other possibility is that a lot of people have something to hide. The peculiarly hysterical tone adopted by many otherwise reasonable persons when discussing privacy, then, is easily understandable: They are afraid of being caught.

The second hypothesis brings to mind a remark by the cartoonist Scott Adams, in his book *The Dilbert Future:* "In the future, new technology will allow the police to solve 100 per cent of all crimes. The bad news is that we'll realize 100 per cent of the population are criminals, including the police." The major source of the moral panic that is the privacy scare, I have come to believe, is the apprehension of many Americans that a truly sophisticated system of camera surveillance and computer information collection will catch them doing things that are technically illegal or, if legal, personally embarrassing. The emotional electricity that crackles around the privacy issue comes from fear of public exposure and humiliation.

Public vs. Private Lives

Every society suffers from the gap between its professed social code and the actual norms of everyday life. Those who try to live strictly according to the code are generally considered annoying prudes; those who openly reject the code are usually treated as probable subversives. Most of us are hypocrites. We pay lip service to the public norms, while frequently flouting them and tolerating considerable deviation in others. Mature, worldly-wise people will look the other way as long as you do not, as the saying goes, frighten the horses.

But the compromise of hypocrisy, in order to succeed, requires a considerable degree of secrecy. (Perhaps the privacy debate should be renamed the secrecy debate.) Once some behavior that is tacitly permitted yet theoretically forbidden is exposed, the public norm is reaffirmed by moral denunciation or at least ridicule of the unfortunate victim.

The catalog of attitudes and actions that are acceptable in secret but unacceptable in public changes constantly. In 1901, illegitimacy or black or Jewish ancestry could be the shocking secret on which a tragic novel turned. In 1951, it was more likely to be homosexuality or a secret divorce. Today's American elite are far more relaxed about all these subjects, to the consternation of conservatives. Nevertheless, the baby boomers and their children have their own morality, and thus their own set of shocking secrets.

It may no longer be disgraceful to have premarital sex, or (in most educated circles) to be homosexual. But the revelation that you are having an extramarital affair, or trolling the Internet for sex partners using the alias Stud Muffin, or perhaps Miss Behavior, would still be highly embarrassing. That alone, I would wager, goes a long way toward explaining the enthusiasm of law-abiding, upright citizens—particularly men—for computer encryption techniques. They are not worried that the FBI or the CIA will discover they are plotting to overthrow the United States. They are worried that their wives will discover their favorite porn sites, or that the FBI agent doing the background check for a Commerce Department job will discover the alias Stud Muffin.

A similar explanation probably underlies the widespread resistance to the introduction of biometric cameras on street corners and in airports. This is not a tool whose intrinsic value reasonable people can disagree on. Cameras that compare faces to photographs in computer databases are a proven and reliable method of identifying criminals and terrorists. The deployment of 250,000 of them in Great Britain has been an extraordinary success; in Glasgow, Scotland, alone they are credited with reducing crime nearly 70 percent. Had a proper system of biometric cameras been in place in American airports on September 11, the World Trade Center towers might be standing today.

Respectable People Living in Fear

Why, then, would anyone except a neo-Confederate militiaman in Idaho or a member of the anarchist Left oppose the adoption of so potent a security weapon in the United States? Here, I think, the opposition has to do with the unacknowledged but widespread consumption of recreational drugs—chiefly marijuana, but also cocaine and more exotic substances like heroin and ecstasy. The enormous market for drugs in the U.S. probably includes people most of us would not ever suspect—the secretary, the corporate vice president, the business school professor (perhaps even you, dear reader).

Those respectable secret drug users must live in fear that biometric cameras will photograph them buying drugs from a dealer or a friend in a public place and automatically alert the local vice squad. I have no proof that this accounts for the near panic the device inspires among many individuals who belong to the educated professions and business community. But it seems a reasonable inference, reinforced by the curious lack of alarm about the use of cameras in apartment and office buildings, where no illicit transactions are likely to take place.

The gap between our public personas and our private weaknesses would merely be fodder for sociological analysis or satire or perhaps literary tragedy, if it were not so potentially dangerous. Should enough elite Americans who are afraid of being photographed buying marijuana on a street corner join forces with radical libertarians to prevent the adoption of biometric cameras in public places, an opportunity will be lost to prevent, or punish, many muggings, murders and acts of political terrorism. On a different but no less relevant plane, should enough elite Americans who are afraid of having someone discover their cosmetic surgery or use of Viagra or Prozac lobby Congress to install extreme medical privacy laws, many of us with treatable diseases and conditions that might have been discovered by the dissemination of medical data would suffer or die unnecessarily.

The Need for Tolerance

If I am correct, terrorists and criminals have found unwitting allies in a large number of Americans who are so worried about the possible exposure of their minor vices or medical conditions that they support a privacy regime which would weaken the ability of government to combat terror and crime. This is actually nothing new. During Prohibition, mainstream Americans who liked a drink now and then were the de facto allies of gangsters. In the case of Prohibition, the tension between the ideal of abstinence from alcohol and the practice of widespread drinking was resolved in favor of the practice. Perhaps a similar approach is needed for many of the behaviors that Americans feel obliged to conceal.

Much of the resistance to biometric cameras might be eliminated if minor vices were legalized, or if prosecutors made it clear that victimless (and propertyless) crimes caught on camera would rarely be prosecuted. Ditto extending the kind of social tolerance already shown toward premarital sex to the use of personal ads, potency-enhancing drugs, cosmetic surgery, and the consumption of pornography—all practices that remain taboo.

At present the dinner conversation of the chattering classes tends to revolve around abs and low-carb diets. The boundaries of crassness would not be pushed much further if someone casually said, "This is

Mary, whom I met in the Bondage and Submission chat room." (We already suspect that many of the couples we know did not meet in the circumstances they describe.)

One of the slogans of the '60s was, "The issue is not the issue." In many of today's heated arguments about privacy, the issue is not the issue either. The privacy debate is being driven by something nobody discusses: changing conceptions of shame in our society. Until we recognize this, it will continue to be a surrogate for another, and perhaps more important, debate.

CHAPTER 4

FREEDOM OF EXPRESSION

THE HISTORICAL FOUNDATION OF FREE SPEECH

Robert Hargreaves

The diverse range of issues that fall under the general term *free speech* have been in the public eye for hundreds of years. In 1644, for example, the English scholar John Milton posited that free speech is important because it leads to the discovery of truth: "Let her and falsehood grapple, for whoever knew truth put to the worse in a free and equal encounter." Robert Hargreaves examines this classic—and often quoted—defense of free speech, as well as other historical justifications for unfettered self-expression. Collectively, these arguments for strong speech protections helped pave the way for the modern—and still evolving—conception of free speech. Hargreaves is the author of *The First Freedom: A History of Free Speech*, from which the following is excerpted.

Progress towards establishing a universal principle of free speech has been neither as even nor inevitable as once supposed. Indeed, it is worth remembering that for much of human history the very concept of 'free speech' would have been quite meaningless. Even in democratic Athens, the liberty of speech so extolled by Pericles was put forward more as a civic duty than as a 'right' in the modern sense of the word. Two thousand years later, when the conditions for civil liberty were again beginning to take shape, the precursors of that liberty had other, quite different, objectives in mind. Neither [religious reformer Martin] Luther nor Galileo [astronomer who was punished for not supporting an Earth-centered universe] ever thought of 'free speech', even as he accidentally advanced it. Later still, when free speech did begin to emerge as a principle to be defined and defended, the arguments put forward in [John] Milton's *Areopagitica*, [John] Locke's *Letter on Toleration*, [James] Madison's Bill of Rights and [John Stuart] Mill's *On Liberty* were, in spite of superficial similarities, arguments for different things, in pursuit of different aims in entirely different circumstances. In the middle of a civil war, Milton sought the liberty of unlicensed printing for Protestant intellectuals like himself; Locke was concerned to distinguish between political and religious rights; Madison strove to limit the power of the new federal government; Mill set out to establish a sweeping general principle that may, or may not, be as relevant today as it was when he wrote it. While there are important lessons to be learned from them all care must be taken not to project their ideas too literally into the present. As the great nineteenth century historian, Leopold von Ranke, taught, every historical age is 'immediate to God'. So it is with individuals. Their contributions to the modern concept of free speech must be judged by their own lights, used by us when they are relevant, while recognising that the ruling passions of one age are not necessarily those of another. If it is to endure, free speech must never become mere 'dead dogma', an inheritance from the past that needs no further examination. It is, after all, part of the principle itself that the best-warranted beliefs must be constantly tested in the crucible of criticism. Reliance on past authority is never enough. The freedoms of the mind, including that of free speech, need to be continually examined, expanded and revitalised in order to determine their current validity.

Multiple Notions of Free Speech

What is clear from an examination of the past is that not one but several notions of what is loosely called 'free speech' exist, related to one another and in many ways interdependent, but each with its own distinct character and pedigree. The struggle to establish the liberty of conscience, for instance, was conducted independently from the struggle for a free press and based on quite different arguments. Then again, the nature of the free enquiry needed to establish a scientific truth is different in kind from the freedom needed by a politician to get his ideas accepted in the democratic marketplace. Does the right to free speech extend to the visual arts? Some have said not, and continue to censor various forms of visual expression in the name of sexual morality. Is television covered by the same principle that guarantees the freedom of the press? Judging by the regulatory framework surrounding most television systems, the answer, at least for the moment, is no.

Another question that then arises is that of the *quality* of the speech to be protected. Are the tabloid newspapers as worthy of protection as a learned dissertation in *The Economist*? Is an impartial source of news more valuable than commercial advertising? Is a book worth fighting for and a comic not? When it comes to art, Picasso's banned *Guernica* and Shostakovich's outlawed symphonies are clearly easier to defend than *The Chain Saw Massacre*, though perhaps not so much because they are a higher form of art, but because banning them was designed to prevent people being politically influenced by them. The question is further complicated when an act of communication is coupled with another sort of conduct—aggressive picketing of non-union workers during a strike, for instance. Clearly, what is at stake here is more the 'freedom of expression' than 'free speech', though the two concepts are often conjoined. In short, the generic term 'free speech' is colloquially used to cover a diverse range of freedoms, each subject to its own definition and its own type of defence or justification.

The Argument from Truth

The classic defence of free speech, going back to Milton, is that it is important first and foremost because it leads to the discovery of truth. 'Let her and falsehood grapple,' Milton wrote in his *Areopagitica*, 'for whoever knew truth put to the worse in a free and equal encounter?' Mill picked up the same argument: open discussion, freedom of enquiry and the interplay of competing beliefs will inexorably lead truth to reveal herself. More recently, the search for truth has been likened to the process of cross-examination in a court of law. When all opinions have been freely heard, the jury of public opinion will deliver its verdict and pick the version of truth it prefers. [Supreme Court Justice] Oliver Wendell Holmes believed the best test of the truth of an idea was to get itself accepted in the competition of the market. His colleague, [Justice] Felix Frankfurter, made a similar point when he said, 'the history of civilisation is in considerable measure the displacement of error which once held sway as official truth by beliefs which have in turn yielded to other truths'. Man's liberty to search for truth should, therefore, remain unfettered 'no matter what orthodoxies he may challenge'. In all these formulations, the right to free speech is not put forward as an end in itself but as a means towards something else: the discovery of truth, which is held to be the dominant good. The process is seamless; truth is simply what for the moment survives until a greater truth comes along to replace it. There are no absolutes.

Modern philosophers find the formulation unconvincing. It fails to give a clear answer to the critical question—does truth *always* emerge triumphant when sent out to grapple with falsehood? Where is the empirical evidence that in every argument reason will prevail? They point to the example of pre-war Germany, where the Nazis put forward views about the racial inferiority of the Jews that were widely accepted. Does this then make their theories true? One hopes not. What survives as a truth in the marketplace is just as likely to lead to error, ignorance, folly or even to unspeakable crimes. There is therefore no link in logic between the right to free speech and an increase in human knowledge and understanding. At best, truth may emerge from a seminar of intellectuals trained to think rationally. That is by no means the same as saying it will prevail when subject to the scrutiny of the public at large. People are not nearly so rational as the leaders of the eighteenth-century Enlightenment assumed who first articulated the idea of rationality. Their optimistic naiveté has long since been discredited by history and bitter experience. Without this assumption, the empirical support for the argument from truth evaporates. As [poet John] Pope said:

The ruling passion be it what it will,
The ruling passion conquers reason still.

Free Speech in the Marketplace of Ideas

Clearly then, there are major flaws in basing a theory of free speech on the assumption that reason will always prevail. But while the freedom to express contrary views may not always lead to truth, it does have another, perhaps more important virtue. By focussing on human fallibility, it posits the admission in every argument that 'I may be wrong and you may be right'. Indeed, in most arguments, I am very likely to be wrong. I therefore need my free speech in order to test my opinion against yours. Even when I reject it, your thought has then helped to shape my thought. This process is especially valuable when applied to matters of ethics, morals and politics, where there is little consensus and, consequently, a large risk of suppressing an opinion which may later turn out to be the right one. That is why the classic defence of free speech based on the collision of competing ideas has been held so strongly and for so many years. What is true and what is false, what is right and what is wrong, what is sound and what is foolish are, in these fields at least, essentially subjective judgements. And if individuals can be fallible in these matters, then so too can those who rule over them. Just as we are properly sceptical about our own ability to distinguish truth from error, so should we be even more sceptical about the motives and abilities of those to whom we grant political power. The treatment meted out to Socrates [the Athenian philosopher who was sentenced to death for objecting to government], Galileo [who was forced to recant his views on the structure of the solar system], [John] Lilburne [an agitator for English constitutional reform who was imprisoned for life], [John] Wilkes and [William] Cobbett [two Englishmen who, on separate occassions, criticized England's government and were subsequently censured], the prosecutions for seditious libel of those now regarded as heroes, the banning of [James Joyce's novel] *Ulysses* and *Guernica*, [FBI chief J. Edgar] Hoover's persecution of dissidents and countless acts of petty censorship are proof enough that authority is a spectacularly bad arbiter in matters of free speech. While not infallible, the free exchange of competing ideas is likely to get nearer to the truth than is any governmental agency. Even when he is wrong, Galileo's enquiring mind is preferable to the dogma of the Inquisition [that charged him with heresy for his view on a sun-centered solar system].

It must, however, be conceded that a defence of free speech based on the collision of competing ideas is unlikely to achieve all that Voltaire, [Thomas] Jefferson and Mill hoped it would. It demonstrably does not always lead to the truth. And even though it retains its validity as a negative justification of free speech—in the sense that it assumes the fallibility of human judgement—it does not provide a justification for the right to free speech in all circumstance. In particular, it does not begin to address the question of the liberty of conscience or the freedom of the press. In order to defend those categories of free speech, other arguments are needed.

The Argument from Democracy

One of the strongest of these arguments is that free speech is necessary to the proper working of democracy. In a sense this goes back to the *isêgoria* of ancient Athens, the right whereby 'free born men, having to advise the public, may speak free'. However, it must always be remembered that for the vast bulk of intervening history, democracy was not a highly regarded form of government. Until two centuries ago, it was associated with mob rule and dark, almost fathomless threats from the lower orders. The ruling classes of Europe and the leaders of the Church looked on it with oligarchic disdain, as did the American Federalists. Not until the days of Jefferson and Madison did it achieve anything like political respectability, and even by the 1930s less than half the countries of Europe could claim to be self-ruling liberal democracies. In most of the non-western world the concept was quite unknown.

It is only where democracy has taken root that a coherent principle of free speech can be based upon it—and then only in genuinely democratic societies that choose their rulers from opposing political parties through elections open to all, by agreement and without violence. This is an argument for free speech that was simply unavailable in the era of Milton, Locke and Voltaire. Even in the early days of the American republic, it took several decades of controversy before they felt able to discard the notion of seditious libel, the belief that governments should be protected from criticism, even during a hotly fought election campaign. Before then, the law in both Britain and America held that governments could be criminally assaulted by mere words and opinions. Any comment about the established order that tended to lower it in the public's esteem was seditious libel, subjecting its author to criminal prosecution. Freedom of speech protected debates in Parliament from encroachments by the crown. It did not give the individual citizen the right to speak his mind. Freedom of the press simply meant the absence of prior restraint, the liberty to print without a licence and answer for the consequences.

Free speech became a necessary civil liberty only after the people themselves became the source of sovereignty, the masters rather than the servants of government. But once that had occurred, the political argument in its favour became irresistible. For a sovereign electorate to choose between rival political parties, it must have an unimpeded supply of information on which to base that choice. Because people cannot intelligently cast their votes without access to the relevant arguments, to deny them access to those arguments is as serious an infringement of their democratic rights as denying them the vote. Furthermore, because a democracy's leaders are answerable to the people, free speech is needed to keep them under constant critical scrutiny. The freedom to criticise government policy and officials, which used to be regarded as seditious libel, is actually a necessary check on the power of elected politicians. Without it, democracy itself would become corrupted. In a modern society, it is, as [social critic] Walter Lippmann once observed, not so much a privilege as an organic necessity.

There is, however, a paradox at the heart of this argument. Democracy is, in essence, rule by the majority. But the right to free speech entails allowing an individual to put forward an unpopular or even a hated idea which the majority might wish to suppress. As we have seen, decisions taken by majorities can be as wrong and tyrannical as those taken by an individual despot. In classical times, a democracy voted to put Socrates to death for expressing his dissent and Horace spoke of *'civium ardor prava jubentium'*, which can be translated as 'the frenzy of the citizens in urging what is wrong'. [A French observer of American democracy, Alexis] de Tocqueville coined the phrase 'tyranny of the majority' and Mill used it to expound his own views on free speech. To take it for granted that free speech comes as part and parcel of democracy is clearly mistaken. What then can be done?

If it is accepted that free speech is vital to the working of democracy, the only way to resolve the paradox is by granting it special protection, to shield it from encroachment even by the sovereign will of an otherwise all-powerful people. This can be justified on the grounds that to deny a minority point of view the right to be heard removes the moral basis for accepting the decisions of the majority. The law of the land then loses its authority and people will not feel bound by decisions from which they have been excluded. Democracy can function effectively only if the majority grant minorities the right to dissent. They need their freedom of speech in order to persuade others to share their point of view. It therefore merits a privileged status. In this case, at least, liberty takes precedence over democracy.

CENSORSHIP IS HARMFUL TO SOCIETY

Nan Levinson

The First Amendment to the Constitution of the United States declares that "Congress shall make no law . . . abridging the freedom of speech." While most Americans claim to embrace their constitutional right to express themselves—and indeed few countries have adopted such expansive free speech protections—the public remains deeply divided over what acts, such as flag desecration or sex on the Internet, constitute protected self-expression. In her book *Outspoken: Free Speech Stories*, Nan Levinson examines the tenuous nature of free speech and describes why she opposes censorship, even in response to speech or expressive acts that some may consider harmful or obscene. According to Levinson, censorship is not only inimical to personal freedom, it is also, in a more practical sense, ineffective and even counterproductive: Banning unpopular political views, for example, does not eradicate them but merely drives them underground.

[Playwright and social critic] Oscar Wilde claimed that whenever people talked about the weather, he felt sure they were really talking about something else. I share that suspicion when it comes to censorship and suspect too that we fight over words and pictures because it is easier to make rules than to make changes. It is also safer, which is why speech battles are usually about problems and resentments we don't know how, or are afraid, to talk about.

Though a good portion of recent attempts to censor have been stopped by the courts, community pressure, or good sense, these fights leave a bad taste in everyone's mouth, and treating lawsuits as a kind of twelve-step recovery program is not a particularly good use of anyone's resources. Moreover, to understand or account for something is not to render it harmless. Measures to control speech confuse a policing action with a political one, and it is not a giant step from policing words to policing people. "Chilling effects" and "slippery slopes," those icy threats brandished in the face of bad laws and policies, are cause for genuine concern, as we are reminded whenever we

Nan Levinson, *Outspoken: Free Speech Stories*. Berkeley: University of California Press, 2003. Copyright © 2003 by Nan Levinson. Reproduced by permission.

stop our bickering long enough to listen for those voices that have been stifled in countries around the globe and throughout history.

Tolerance Is an Acquired Taste

Many would-be censors are cynics, fanatics, or spoilsports, but those bent on doing good can present as great a threat to free speech and thought. Blaming words is a way to whittle stubborn social dilemmas down to a manageable size. It lets us feel as if we're doing something, even if that something is investing symbols with the power to make the improvements that we can't. And feeling right and righteous among the like-minded is comforting and exciting, as anyone who has ever advocated a cause knows. So for all their virulence, there is something poignant in campaigns to control TV programs because we can't control our kids' behavior, in attempts to remove books from libraries because we can't make sex less powerful in life, in bans on ethnic slurs because we haven't resolved the question that plagues us from our first foray onto the playground of what to do when someone says something rotten to us and it hurts.

Even for those who don't take up morality as a hobby, what we are asked to stomach in the name of free speech can seem like too much: a culture that assaults the senses and talk that is so cheap it might as well be free because no one in his right mind would pay for it. The temptation to squash vexing speech comes in the specific instance too. When someone says something that upsets us, making him or her stop offers more immediate and tangible satisfaction than the idea of free speech. Self-protection is innate, tolerance an acquired taste.

Then too, words have weight and consequences. If we didn't believe that, why all the fuss over what we can and can't say? Separate from any action it may bring about, language contributes to an atmosphere, and contrary to the children's rhyme, names can hurt or scare or disgust us. We may know that words and pictures are representations, not the thing itself, know that tolerating a message is not the same as agreeing with it, know too that should we come across something unbidden and unappealing on TV or a computer, we can turn it off or turn away. And still, words haunt. Underlying the intolerance of words is the fear, justified or manufactured, that our society is coming apart at the seams. Speech codes, cyberfilters, stamp-out-smut drives, curriculum restrictions, and other attempts to hobble expression are a direct response to that fear, as if all our talk about talk will keep the lid on an explosive situation.

Why Fight It?

I confess to a little envy here. Being able to speak without official sanction has always seemed such a basic and glorious need to me that I would like to be as certain as the speech blamers appear to be, but what I am, more often, is baffled. For instance, it seems clear that mean, ugly epithets are a form of racism that interferes with people's freedom. But humankind has spent millennia figuring out ways to discriminate against some of its members, and most of those ways undermine much more effectively than invective. So while I don't know how to end racism, I suspect that it won't be by rewriting the dictionary.

Or this: I can make a long list of things I really don't want to see or hear, but I still don't understand how anyone can believe that getting rid of pornography or off-color jokes will improve her life in any significant way. (On the other hand, equal pay for women, adequate health care, and universal literacy, to name just three concrete goals, would get us much closer to the feminist aims of fairness and groceries, and if we put the same effort into achieving these as we have into arguing over pictures, they might just come to pass.) Still, a lot of people do believe passionately that antiporn campaigns will help them, so I'm left to figure that they believe it because they want to. It is a leap of faith, then, which is why I've come to understand that repeating arguments against censorship will not eradicate it any more than censorship will eradicate the evils it is said to fight.

Yet arguments for free speech must be made. Otherwise, it all comes down to who hollers loudest. Free speech gets defended on two fronts: for the principle and for the expression itself. When I can't bring myself to do the latter, I take refuge in the former; hence, my arguments with censorship are both philosophical and practical.

First, being able to speak our minds makes us feel good. True, we tailor our words to civility, persuasion, kindness, or other purposes, but that is our choice. Censors claim the right to purge other people's talk—all the while insisting that it is for our own good.

Second, much censorship appears irrational and alarmist in retrospect because the reasons people choose and use words are vastly more interesting than the systems designed to limit them. It's not hard to make a list of absurdities—I'm particularly fond of a rash of state laws that forbid the disparagement of agricultural products—but simplistic explanations and simple-minded responses are as dangerous as they are ditzy. In one of the few places that postmodern theory and common sense intersect, it is obvious that the meaning and perception of words regularly depend on such variables as speaker and spoken to, individual experience and shared history, and the setting, company, and spirit in which something is said. To give courts or other authorities the power to determine all this is, to put it mildly, mind-boggling.

Third, censorship is inimical to democracy. Cloaking ideas and information in secrecy encourages ignorance, corruption, demagoguery, a corrosive distrust of authority, and a historical memory resembling Swiss cheese. Open discussion, on the other hand, allows verities to be examined, errors to be corrected, disagreement to be expressed, and anxieties to be put in perspective. It also forces communities to confront their problems directly, which is more likely to lead to real solutions than covering them up.

Fourth, censorship backfires. Opinions, tastes, social values, and mores change over time and vary among people. Truth can be a protean thing. The earth's rotation, its shape, the origins of humankind, and the nature of matter were all once widely understood to be something different from what we know today, yet those who challenged the prevailing faith were mocked and punished for their apostasy. Banning ideas in an attempt to make the world safe from doubt, disaffection, or disorder is limiting, especially for people whose lives are routinely limited, since the poor and politically weak are the censor's first targets.

Finally, censorship doesn't work. It doesn't get rid of bad ideas or bad behavior. It usually doesn't even get rid of bad words, and history has shown repeatedly that banning the unpalatable merely drives it underground. It could be argued that that's just fine, that vitriolic or subversive speech, for example, shouldn't dare to speak its name. But hateful ideas by another name—disguised as disinterested intellectual inquiry, or given a nose job like Ku Klux Klansman David Duke before he ran for governor of Louisiana—are probably more insidious than those that are clearly marginal.

An Impossible Task

The problem is that it is just not practically possible to outlaw only the bad words and leave the good ones unscathed. We may be able to make a list of words or phrases that could be dropped from the language with no significant loss of expressiveness or communication. Profanity, epithets, and adolescent nasties don't contribute much to debate, the pursuit of truth, self-knowledge, or the practice of democracy, the things the framers of the Constitution appeared to have in mind when they sought to safeguard expression. But banned words get replaced by equally offensive ones with a speed that makes our heads whirl. People who want to affront and wound will find a way to do so, no matter how they are constrained, and people who offend inadvertently (probably all of us at one time or another) can be corrected in other, less drastic and more constructive ways.

The alternative to spelling out what is not allowed is to fashion a vague statement of intent and then determine what speech is forbidden on a case-by-case basis. But, with the possible exception of an antinudity ordinance in Florida that took 346 words to define *buttocks*, these statements are inevitably too narrow or too broad. More important, the decisions will always be made by people in positions of control, and those who hope sanitized speech will bring about greater justice are well advised not to trust the powerful to help them out. History is fickle, and nowhere does power give itself up willingly.

There may be much the founding fathers didn't anticipate about

America two centuries later, but they were prescient and self-interested enough to craft the First Amendment, which is still admirable for its elegant simplicity, for its defiance of pettiness, and for what it tries to do. What the First Amendment tries to do is support the shut up, the shoved aside, the left out, and the picked on. An anomaly in the mythology of our American selves, it allows us, on occasion, to win arguments with words and expressiveness instead of bank accounts and bullets. It doesn't set up an official truth, but it offers our best hope for getting to some public truth over time. The First Amendment is integral to forging the common awareness that is key to the functioning of democracy, and it suggests a way to bridge the growing gap between the autonomy we cherish and the community we need if we're to live in any sort of harmony. (It certainly illuminates that gap like a sound and light show over the Grand Canyon.) Finally, in its own roundabout way, the First Amendment gives muscle to the idea that what is best about America needs not just praise but also protection, and scrutiny, and honest appraisal.

A character in a story by Grace Paley rails against dumbness, which she defines as "silence and stupidity." "By silence," Paley writes, "she meant the refusal to speak; by stupidity she meant the refusal to hear." The First Amendment may be a whistle in the dark of dumbness, but it is where we begin.

SOME CENSORSHIP IS BENEFICIAL TO SOCIETY

Jonah Goldberg

Jonah Goldberg, a nationally syndicated columnist and editor of *National Review Online*, has written extensively on politics and culture. In Goldberg's view, society has been brainwashed into thinking that censorship is always a threat to personal liberty. In truth, according to Goldberg, the right to express oneself is neither unassailable nor absolute. Although often misinterpreted, according to Goldberg, the First Amendment does not preclude the regulation of expression, such as child pornography, that may degrade society. That many forms of useful censorship exist, writes Goldberg, is incontrovertible: Children's Saturday morning television, for example, does not include programming that is obscene or sexually graphic.

Censorship. This is perhaps the most powerful abracadabra word in the world. Unlike, say, Rumpelstiltskin's name—which you had to mention at least once—you don't even need to say the word "censorship" to conjure torrents of cheap patriotism, pugnacious ignorance, and widespread panic about the future of freedom itself. All you need do is speak in the most modestly positive tones about the idea that there are some things which should be—shudder—banned, and Hollywood goes into a Chinese fire-drill of outrage, the ACLU cancels all staff vacations, and Republicans cower under their desks lest someone accuse them of being—shudder, shudder—prudes. Indeed, in terms of the political culture of this country, the only thing that is truly censored is any discussion of the merits of censorship.

Even the most successful censors, the speech-code radicals and vandal-apologists on college campuses, can't admit that they are in favor of censorship. Whenever a bunch of morons burn some conservative newspapers, the deans and teachers bend so far backwards to explain that burning newspapers is "a form of expression too," you'd expect they'd be able to self-administer a proctological exam.

When some white kid says something nice about the British Empire or [conservative Israeli prime minister] Ariel Sharon—or even utters the names of Charles Murray [author of *The Bell Curve*], Dinesh D'Souza, or David Horowitz [other prominent conservative authors] without spitting up bile—he's tossed into some reeducation cubicle to watch videos about tolerance. Gay radicals, black activists, and feminists with rice-paper-thin skins want to create vast categories of "hate crimes" and harassment laws that would in effect outlaw all sorts of speech. But no one dares call any of this "censorship."

In fact, if even these objectively pro-censorship lefties said they favored censorship, they'd probably lose their jobs, or at least get into trouble. You can write a million words on various loves that dare not speak their names, but say one nice thing about censorship and, according to the *New York Times*, you are a Nazi or, worse, [former attorney general] John Ashcroft.

Censorship, in Principle

Well, let me just say, even though I'm opposed to today's campus censorship: I do like censorship. I wish there was more of it. I wish we could talk about it. I wish we could have an argument about it. And the first thing necessary for that argument is to rescue it from its status as the pointy-headed equivalent of a "fighting word."

Call me a junior member of the Old White Conservatives Club. Irving Kristol, Robert Bork, and Walter Berns [conservative scholars well known for their positions against First Amendment speech protections] have been arguing in favor of censorship for close to 40 years (Kristol calls it the "Walter Berns–Robert Bork–Irving Kristol Club," but that's not a club I would presume to join uninvited. It'd be like unilaterally chiseling my face on Mount Rushmore). Writing in *The Weekly Standard* a few years ago, Irving Kristol noted that lots of respected thinkers admit that the pro-censorship folks have the better argument. They even say they agree with Kristol & co. "in principle."

"'In principle' must rank among the saddest phrases in the English language," Kristol lamented. "When someone says he agrees with you in principle, that is usually prefatory to his explaining that he disagrees with you in fact."

So let's stick with the principle first.

Some things are inappropriate, awful, or just plain evil. We all agree on this. By "we" I mean the people not reflexively determined to be clever no matter how obnoxiously stupid it makes them sound. If ABC devoted the Sunday dinner hour to a hardcore triple-X orgy, we'd say, "That's inappropriate."

If Princeton "ethicist" Peter Singer made a movie graphically illustrating his conviction that there's nothing wrong whatsoever for people to get jiggy with a sheep or orangutan, and the MPAA [Motion Picture Association of America] gave it a G-rating, we'd say, "That's awful."

And if you actually saw child pornography—anywhere, at any time, in any place—you'd say, "That's evil."

The reason we don't see things like this is that we already *have* censorship in this country. We've always had censorship in this country. Indeed, it's easy to denounce censorship when you are blind to the fact that it already exists all around us. And, since it exists, it's pointless to say you are against if you really aren't. Unless you believe that the state has no right to stop the most debased things from appearing on your kids' Saturday-morning TV, you already believe in the "principle" of censorship. The question is how much and where you believe that principle should be applied.

Hollywood liberals, who claim that censorship is never warranted, make fools of themselves every time they open their mouths. Jack Valenti [chairman and CEO of the Motion Picture Association] and [actor] Alec Baldwin can always be relied upon to say there's no evidence that sex or violence have any adverse effects on people. But they also believe, rightly, that art can be uplifting—that it makes us better people when exposed to it. Well, as Irving Kristol noted long ago, if you believe that a book or a movie can't hurt people, you also pretty much have to believe a book or a movie can't help them either.

Look: If TV can't influence people, how come I can't watch NBC for more than few minutes without being force-fed some public-service treacle about how "hate" is bad or why beating your wife is wrong? Why bother—if TV can't teach?

Harm, Shmarm

This illustrates the problem with the censorship "debate" today. The standard for what should or shouldn't be censored has moved entirely from the moral to the utilitarian (for the record, *some* utilitarianism is always useful).

Recently, I wrote about child pornography both in my syndicated column and for NRO [*National Review Online*], and ever since I've been getting e-mail from people across the ideological spectrum shrieking at me about my support for banning "thought crimes." Basically, I criticized the attorney general for accepting the notion that anti-kiddie porn needs to be "proved" harmful before it can be banned. To be fair to Ashcroft, I'm sure he agrees that it's absurd that the government should have to prove harm before it can ban even virtual depictions of men having sex with five-year-olds. I called this a "sick joke" and wrote that "some things just deserve to be censored because they are evil."

For this I've been getting endless grief from the sorts of people who think shouting the cliché, "I may disagree with what you say but I will defend to the death your right to say it!" is the height of sophistication. In effect, my critics think that my willingness to forbid people access to images of graphic sex between kids, or between kids and adults—so long as it's all make-believe—makes me a totalitarian.

Rather than cite splenetic e-mails, I refer you instead to the more thoughtfully composed exposition of this foolishness by *Washington Post* columnist William Raspberry.

Raspberry, like my correspondents, believes that my position—that we can ban the obviously evil—is "dangerous to our constitutional liberties."

It may be. But if we never do anything that is dangerous, a lot of important things will never get done. War is dangerous to our civil liberties. Social Security, the income tax, driver's licenses, interstate highways, gun control, affirmative action, farm subsidies, environmental regulations, the Americans with Disabilities Act, campaign-finance "reform," food-safety regulation: All of these things and many, many other governmental actions are "dangerous" to our constitutional liberties. Some of these things are quite worthwhile, others less so. Some aren't even potentially, theoretically, hypothetically, or otherwise-abstractly dangerous to our constitutional liberties. Others can actually be shown to have done grievous and permanent damage to our constitutional liberties.

In other words, why does constitutional purity only occur to civil libertarians when the question is whether or not we should protect deviant, disgusting, and patently evil "speech"? The serious libertarians, who are "pure" on all of these other issues, can speak without hypocrisy about slippery slopes and the dangers to constitutional liberty. Indeed, I salute them!

Everybody else should shut up.

E Pluribus Porn

More to the point, for the vast majority of this nation's history it was entirely uncontroversial to say child pornography—and lots of much tamer stuff—should be censored. In fact, it would be considered controversial to suggest it was an open question.

Why on earth should we have to conduct a thousand studies around the country in order to "prove" that kiddie porn is harmful? Do we really lack the moral and intellectual self-confidence to simply assert the obvious? Spare me the lectures that we banned other things that we thought were bad, only to embrace them later. We're not talking about "other things"; we're talking about Child Pornography. I'd love to debate censoring "other things" later, but let's talk about the easy stuff first.

Radical academics *want* to have these arguments and these studies precisely because they know that the more we talk about bestiality, the more we rationalize perversion, and the more we pooh-pooh the "moral panic" over pedophilia, the more likely we will be to define deviancy down. As [philosopher Jean-Jacques] Rousseau noted, "Vice hardly insinuates itself by shocking decency, but by taking on its likeness."

Whenever I read about Peter Singer's views on interspecies dating, for example, I think of [conservative columnist] William F. Buckley's famous retort, "I would like to take you seriously but to do so would affront your intelligence."

You don't have to dust off your books by William Bennett [writer and speaker known for his conservative stance on moral issues] and George Will [conservative syndicated columnist] to understand that it is an indisputable fact that the Founding Fathers believed the good character of the citizenry was essential to a healthy republic. And, they believed, laws crafted at the local level—including censorship—could and should be aimed at maintaining good character.

And therein lay the hitches. First of all, for a bunch of reasons, local communities have a harder time censoring things. First, there's the market. TV is a national medium. The Internet is a global medium. It's very difficult to set a "community standard" when the community stretches across a continent (yeah, yeah: plus Hawaii) and includes over 270 million people. Or when—in the case of the Internet—the community is the global village (a phrase I promise will not return to this column, without being mocked, for years).

Then there's the law. Because of the Fourteenth Amendment and various other power-grabs by the federal government, federalism and republicanism have been teetering on the edge of the crapper for years. Congress can make laws about what kids should eat in a Philadelphia school cafeteria, or what kind of car someone can drive on a San Diego highway. Whether you like it or not, the United States is becoming one giant community—and that means more, not less, fighting about what the federal government can and should do. On the whole, I think this is too bad for everybody.

Refilling the Tube

But there's one more hitch. The Founders—broadly defined to mean pretty much everyone who ran this country until the 1930s or so—understood that the law was useful for *maintaining* good character. As Rousseau put it, "Censorship can be useful for preserving morals, but never for reestablishing them." Keeping beer from people who've never had booze is comparatively easy. Keeping it from people who agree with Homer Simpson that beer is the temporary solution to all problems is a much trickier proposition.

Once American society comes to believe that there's nothing wrong with something, it is almost impossible to take it away from them. The old saying in Washington about such things is that you can't put the toothpaste back in the tube. This is obviously wrong. It's just that it's extremely difficult to put the paste back, and you'll likely make a huge mess in the process—but that doesn't necessarily mean it's never worth trying.

Regardless, when it comes to sexual matters in our culture, the tube is almost empty. But there are still a last few dregs of toothpaste left in the tube. The biggest clump, closest to the opening, is child pornography. Like it or not, the other side has taken up the fight. Sexual-leftists argue for the "demystification" of what they call "consensual inter-generational sex." On the right, meanwhile, there's a lot of pussyfoot-ing. My wife, who works for the attorney general and has had to deal with this issue more than she'd like, says to me all the time, "If Amer-icans could see the 'harmless' virtual kiddie porn we're talking about, this debate would be over." She's right, and not just in the "yes, dear" sort of way. But, in the absence of such hardball, we have to argue about "harm" and hypothetical dangers to our constitutional liber-ties, and invoke stories of *Tropic of Cancer* [Henry Miller's autobio-graphical novel that was deemed obscene and temporarily banned from publication] being banned as if they're even remotely relevant.

I think it should be censored. Period. You make it, virtual or other-wise, you get in trouble with the law. Use real kids, you definitely go to jail. Use "virtual" kids, you at least should be shut down. But, ulti-mately, I don't care whether it's virtual or real. I don't care what you say on appeal. I don't care if it causes harm. I don't care if you keep it on the farm (sorry, Dr. Seuss rhymes are probably inappropriate here).

By agreeing *now* that it should be censored, we can, following Rousseau's observation, preserve morals without facing a situation where we later have to figure out how to restore them. Leave this tooth-paste in the tube.

INDECENCY IN THE MEDIA SHOULD BE RESTRICTED

Robert Peters

Robert Peters is the president of Morality in the Media, a non-profit organization that promotes decency standards in the media. The following presentation by Peters was given at a 2000 conference on sex and violence in news and entertainment programming. In Peters's view, children are adversely affected by popular media that is rife with lewdness, vulgarity, and other forms of indecency. In response, Peters advocates governmental regulation of the entertainment industry to prevent the indiscriminate distribution of potentially harmful programming. Peters rejects the view that First Amendment protections of speech are absolute; rather, Peters maintains that concern for the common good can and should be balanced with the preservation of personal liberties.

I was born in 1949. Not all was well in the U.S. at that time, but if we compare the rates in the 1950s of teen abortion, premarital sex, sexually transmitted diseases, unwed pregnancies and births, and violent crime, with the rates in the 1990s, we discover that the rates for teens have skyrocketed.

Media Responsibility Is Needed

Clearly, no one cause explains the rise. Since the 1950s there has been a breakdown of authority in the home and public schools. The positive influence of religion has declined. There has been a dramatic increase in use of illegal drugs. The tragic cycle of poverty has taken its toll, as has mental illness.

But it is parents, religious institutions, schools, peers and popular culture that are the primary sources of role models and values for youth. Parents, schools and religious institutions certainly have changed since the 1950s, but few are telling kids it is OK to engage in promiscuous sex and violent crime.

Peers haven't changed much either. They've always been a bad in-

Robert Peters, "Media Responsibility in a Democratic Society," www.moralityinmedia. com, April 10, 2000. Reproduced by permission.

fluence! What has changed drastically in the last 30–40 years has been the content of "popular culture." It is, to shocking degree, more vulgar, more sexual and more violent.

To blame all sexual misbehavior and violent crime on the media would, of course, be absurd, but to say that there is absolutely no causal relationship whatsoever between sex and violence in the media and misbehavior in real life would be equally absurd.

When common sense, personal experience, piles of anecdotal evidence and a substantial body of social science research all point to some sort of causal relationship, the burden of proof should shift to those who say there is no connection.

The Nature of Media Responsibility: Moral and Legal

There are two levels of media responsibility: moral and legal. As defined in *Webster's New World Dictionary* (3rd College Edition, 1988), "moral" means: "relating to, dealing with, or capable of making the distinction between, right and wrong in conduct".

As I see it, it is wrong for Hollywood to churn out films that depict in graphic and often sadistic detail, exploitative deadly violence that is imitable, even by children.

It is wrong for broadcast TV networks to churn out programming that is vulgar and lewd and that provides endless "role models" for sexual promiscuity, adultery and perversion.

It is wrong for cable and satellite TV operators to provide cable versions of hardcore porn films on a pay-per-view basis.

It is wrong for radio stations to broadcast explicit rap lyrics that boast about rape and other sexual abuse of women or to broadcast the gutter talk of "shock jocks" such as Howard Stern.

It is wrong for media news departments to milk almost every sex scandal and horrific crime that comes along for every ratings point that can be extracted from it. Preoccupation with stories that are attention grabbing but which do not inform or educate about important public issues does not serve the public interest. News stories can also beget copycat behavior.

Misconceptions about the First Amendment notwithstanding, there are also legal responsibilities. As [Supreme Court] Justice Brennan put it in *Roth v. United States*, 354 U.S. 476, at 483 (1957):

> "[I]t is apparent that the unconditional phrasing of the First Amendment was not intended to protect every utterance."

Among the various laws that could impact the manner in which sex or violence is portrayed in the media are those governing:

Aiding and abetting a crime
Inciting unlawful conduct

Indecency
Invasion of privacy
Obscenity
Porn Victims' Compensation Act (Illinois)
Sexual exploitation of a child

Two issues that have generated a great deal of discussion in recent years are whether the First Amendment (1) prevents government from regulating media violence to protect children or (2) prevents persons from suing the media for harms suffered because of the irresponsible manner in which violence is depicted.

Protecting Minors

I do not think the First Amendment prevents government from restricting minors' access to entertainment that glamorizes violence causing serious bodily injury or death, no matter how exploitative, gratuitous, graphic and easily imitable it is.

I recognize that drawing lines between speech protected by the First Amendment and speech that is not can present difficulties. But if the Supreme Court, in order to protect adults on the job, can identify forms of "sexual expression" that constitute illegal sexual harassment, the Court, in order to protect children, can also identify forms of media violence that cannot legally be shown to children, at least in the absence of a parent or guardian.

I would add that commercial portrayals of hardcore violence as entertainment and for no other reason than to make a profit, surely lie at the periphery of First Amendment concern [see, e.g., *Miller v. California*, 413 U.S. 15, at 35 (1973)].

Media Liability

I also do not think the First Amendment was intended to shield the media from all responsibility for any and all harms resulting from irresponsible portrayals of violence. In discussing the extent of freedom of the press, the Supreme Court said in *Near v. Minnesota*, 283 U.S. 697, at 713–715 (1931):

> The main purpose of such provisions is "to prevent all such previous restraints upon publications as had been practiced by other governments.". . . They do not prevent subsequent punishment of such as may be deemed contrary to the public welfare. . . . The point of criticism has been "that . . . the liberty of the press might be rendered a mockery . . . if while every man was at liberty to publish what he pleased, the public authorities might nevertheless punish him for harmless publications.". . . But it is recognized that punishment for the abuse of the liberty accorded to the press is essential to the protection of the public, and that the common law rules that

subject the libeler to responsibility for the public offense, as well as the private injury, are not abolished by the protection extended in our constitutions.

The *Near* case focused on libelous material, but in *Chaplinsky v. New Hamphire*, 315 U.S. 568, at 571–572 (1942), the Court elaborated on the scope of First Amendment protection:

> There are certain well-defined and narrowly limited classes of speech, the prevention and punishment of which have never been thought to raise any Constitutional problem. These include the lewd and obscene, the profane, the libelous, and the insulting or "fighting" words—those which by their very utterance inflict injury. . . . It has been well observed that such utterances are no essential part of any exposition of ideas, and are of such slight social value as a step to truth that any benefit that may be derived from them is clearly outweighed by the social interest in order and morality.

While some depictions of media violence (e.g., the slaughter in [*Saving*] *Private Ryan* and *Schindler's List*) are undoubtedly intended to be part of an "exposition of ideas," it is all too clear to any honest observer that much if not most media violence is exploitative, unnecessary and of no "social value."

In saying that I do not think the First Amendment should shield the media from all responsibility for harms resulting from irresponsible portrayals of violence, I do not say the media should be strictly liable. Looking again to libel law, persons who make false defamatory statements can be held liable only if they acted with a lack of care amounting to at least negligence. In some cases involving media, actual malice must be proved.

Furthermore, the law of negligence often aims more at reducing or minimizing risks rather than eliminating them. No matter how responsibly an act of violence is portrayed in the media, there is always a risk that someone could get a "wrong idea" and act on it. Most experts on media violence are not saying that the media should never portray a violent act. They are saying that the manner in which media violence is portrayed can decrease the risks of harm.

Should Living in a "Democratic Society" Make a Difference?

The First Amendment speaks first about the free exercise of religion and then about freedom of speech and of the press. No one argues that the "free exercise" clause guarantees to every American the right to do or say anything, as long as it is motivated by sincere or, perhaps, semi-sincere religious belief.

One well known civil libertarian organization, however, does argue that the First Amendment protects *all* "sexual expression," including child pornography. Civil libertarians are now rising to the defense of "violent expression" with much the same vigor and absolutism that propelled their misguided defense of pornography.

I think the Supreme Court got it right when it rejected the extreme view that First Amendment protection for speech and press is absolute. I think the Court got it right when it recognized that the First Amendment would often require finding a balance between legitimate societal interests and personal freedoms.

I think the majority of Americans are rightly concerned about the effect that media sex and violence is having on society in general and youth in particular. I think they want something done about it—and if the media won't do it, then government should.

But in a "democratic society" such as ours, some compromises may also be necessary. For example, while it may be acceptable for consenting adults to choose to view a particular film or TV program depicting sex or violence, it will often not be acceptable to distribute it to minors or in a manner or in a medium that makes it difficult, if not impossible, for unconsenting adults to avoid. For example, there is a difference between a premium cable TV channel, like HBO, and a basic cable or broadcast TV channel.

There is an old saying, "Your rights end where mine begin." There is a basic human right enjoyed by all Americans, young and old, to live in a safe, healthy and decent society. At present, much of "popular culture" is at war with that right. The media could correct the problems without government intervention, but it is doubtful whether the media will accept the responsibility.

Teaching Media Literacy Is an Alternative to Censorship

Marjorie Heins and Christina Cho

Marjorie Heins coordinates the Free Expression Policy Project (FEPP) at the Brennan Center for Justice at NYU School of Law. She is the author of *Sex, Sin, and Blasphemy: A Guide to America's Censorship Wars* and *Not in Front of the Children: "Indecency," Censorship, and the Innocence of Youth.* In the following FEPP report, Heins and coauthor Christina Cho argue that censorship exercised on behalf of young people is an unsatisfactory response to concerns about the harmful effects of mass media. Rather, the authors advocate media literacy education, an approach that empowers children and adolescents by teaching them how to understand and analyze a prodigious variety of violent, sexual, or otherwise troublesome media messages. Perhaps most importantly, write Heins and Cho, media literacy education not only enables youth to critically evaluate ideas found in popular culture, it also preserves the First Amendment protections that are so basic to a free society.

From the early days of radio and movies to the vast resources of today's World Wide Web, the mass media have been an object of fascination for youth. Yet parents, educators, and youth advocates have long been uneasy about many of the media messages that children and teenagers encounter. Popular culture can glamorize violence, irresponsible sex, junk food, drugs, and alcohol; it can reinforce stereotypes about race, gender, sexual orientation, and class; it can prescribe the lifestyle to which one should aspire, and the products one must buy to attain it.

Thus, it isn't surprising that calls to censor the mass media in the interest of protecting youth have been a mainstay of American politics for many years. Attempts to censor gangster movies in the 1930s, crime comics in the 1950s, and TV violence today have produced an almost unending series of laws, regulations, and proposals for restrict-

Marjorie Heins and Christina Cho, "Media Literacy: An Alternative to Censorship," The Free Expression Policy Project, Fall 2003. Reproduced by permission. For the full report, see www.fepproject.org/policyreportsmedialiteracy.html.

ing the art, information, and entertainment available to youth. The advent of the Internet—a medium in which young people are often better versed than their elders—has only intensified these concerns.

Censorship Is Impractical

There are many reasons why censorship is an unsatisfactory response to concerns about the mass media and its effects on youth. Foremost is the First Amendment, which protects the ability of youngsters as well as adults to read, watch, listen, access ideas, and think about them. This First Amendment protection is not simply a legal technicality to be overcome if possible by laws or policies cleverly crafted to avoid constitutional pitfalls. The right to explore art and ideas is basic to a free society. Without it, children and adolescents cannot grow into the thoughtful, educated citizens who are essential to a functioning democracy.

There are also practical reasons why censorship to "protect" youth is a bad idea. First, it is difficult for people to agree on what should be censored, and to define it in terms that are clear enough to put publishers and distributors on notice of what is banned. Many people point to "violence in the media," "extreme violence," or "gratuitous violence" as inappropriate and harmful to children. But these are elastic and subjective concepts. And most of those who think that "media violence" is bad for kids acknowledge that they don't mean to include televised versions of Shakespeare, Sophocles, or Saving Private Ryan.

Context counts for everything in art and entertainment: how is the violence presented; what are the consequences; what are the ambiguities in the story? There is no way that a censorship law or a simplistic letter-or-number rating system can make these judgments. As media scholar Henry Jenkins has observed, because different youngsters react very differently to the mythology, symbols, and stories in popular entertainment, "universalizing claims are fundamentally inadequate in accounting for media's social and cultural impact."

Censorship also creates taboos that make the forbidden material more attractive. Curious youngsters will defy the bans—making their way into R-rated movies, de-programming v-chips and Internet filters, sneaking looks at dad's Hustler or mom's Playgirl. Indeed, it sometimes seems that censoring youth is more about sending them a message of social disapproval than about actually preventing them from reading or viewing everything that might be thought age-inappropriate or psychologically damaging. But if the idea is to disapprove bad values and inculcate good ones, and more importantly, to teach youngsters how to make these judgments for themselves, then there are more effective ways than censorship to go about it.

Here is where media literacy education comes in. It not only teaches students how media messages are made and how they differ from reality, but it shows them how to analyze those messages, whether they involve commercial advertising, ethnic and gender stereotypes, violence, sexual decision-making, or other complex issues. As a White House report recently noted, media literacy empowers young people, not only to understand and evaluate the ideas found in popular culture, but "to be positive contributors to society, to challenge cynicism and apathy and to serve as agents of social change." Whatever the effectiveness of censorship, it can't accomplish this. Education in media literacy is thus not simply an alternative to censorship; it is far preferable to censorship, for it enhances rather than curtails young people's intellectual growth and their development into critically thinking adults. . . .

What Is Media Literacy Education?

To be media literate is, simply put, to possess the critical thinking skills needed to "read" mass media communications, be they advertisements featuring sophisticated-looking women smoking cigarettes, quick-cut shootout scenes in action films, or coverage of far-off wars on the evening news. Rather than being passive consumers of movies, TV shows, and video games, or looking at them as neutral vehicles for information possessing some valid claim to authority or truth, students learn that media "realities" are "constructed"—whether to produce an adrenalin rush, sell a product, or reflect a social or cultural idea. They may also learn about the economic concentration of today's mass media, and the ways that large media corporations censor and control information.

In the U.S., media literacy education has been incorporated into English language arts, social studies, and health education courses; it is also sometimes a discrete course of study. Most programs include class discussions on media production techniques, narrative elements such as characterization and symbolism, and structure of the media industry. Many supplement classroom lessons with hands-on projects, calling on students to create their own advertisements, public service spots, or video games. After-school programs, youth arts or journalism projects, and church groups also provide media literacy education.

Efforts to introduce media literacy education have been frustrated at times by the notion that popular culture is fundamentally less enriching or edifying than traditional curriculum subjects. At different points in the 1980s and '90s, "back to basics" attitudes took hold in the U.S., Canada, and England—favoring traditional, conservative pedagogy and the avoidance of educational "frills." In these climates, media literacy tends to be one of the first subjects dropped.

But as media literacy leader David Considine writes, the role of mass media "in shaping public perception and public policy" cannot be ignored. He quotes the educator Ernest Boyer: "'it is no longer enough to simply read and write. Students must also become literate in the understanding of visual messages.'" They must learn "'how to spot a stereotype, isolate a social cliche and distinguish facts from propaganda.'"

After decades of relative neglect or sporadic support, the U.S. government today recognizes the importance of media literacy. State education departments have incorporated media literacy and critical thinking in their curricular standards. But the comprehensiveness and sophistication of the different programs around the country vary enormously, and the federal financial commitment is still quite small.

Diverse Approaches to Media Literacy

In the continuing absence of a strong national mandate, various private groups have stepped in to supply information and resources, most often by publishing curricula, conducting training workshops, and organizing conferences. The diversity of these media literacy organizations reflects the multi-faceted concerns of the movement. University-based and scholar-led groups such as the Center for Media Studies at Rutgers University and the Graduate Program in Media Literacy at Appalachian State University are the source of much of the theoretical discourse on media literacy, and also provide information, training, and resources. Citizens for Media Literacy in North Carolina concentrates on the potential for media literacy to foster more active citizenship. The New Mexico Media Literacy Project teaches kids to recognize and resist the consumerism and often addictive behavior promoted by TV advertising. San Francisco's Just Think Foundation targets lower-income youngsters who are deemed "at risk" for crime, violence, or drug use. In 2001, the Alliance for a Media Literate America formed to unite many of these groups, with the goal of "bringing media literacy education to all 60 million students in the United States, their parents, their teachers, and others who care about youth."

The communications industry has not been oblivious to these developments, and some companies have initiated media literacy programs of their own, or have offered funding to media educators. This issue of corporate funding has set off one of the major debates in the media literacy field. TV networks including ABC, CBS, NBC, the Discovery Channel, and, in a highly controversial instance, the commercial provider of classroom news and advertisements, Channel One, have sponsored media literacy projects. The situation is rife with conflict of interest, as corporate-sponsored programs will inevitably steer clear of too-stringent a critique of their benefactors. As Professors Justin Lewis and Sut Jhally say (describing a media literacy program sponsored by Continental Cablevision), the company's notion of "informed citizenship means little more than a weekly perusal of *TV Guide*."

The conflict over corporate sponsorship also highlights a philosophical rift between those who focus on analysis of media content and those who view the structure of the media industry as an equally important concern. Wally Bowen of Citizens for Media Literacy observes that the "structural issue of media ownership" is one of the major challenges for media literacy educators, especially given the increasing consolidation of the communications industry, which is leaving less and less room for grassroots or dissenting voices.

Media literacy leaders also disagree over fundamental objectives. Many oppose the "protectionist" or "inoculationist" philosophy, which sees media education primarily as a way to protect children from bad messages—and in the process, denigrate their favorite TV programs, music videos, and video games. The result, they fear, is decreased student interest and ineffective education. "Many teachers at both the K–12 and university levels have found that students are unresponsive to the idea that they are helpless victims of media influence who need to be rescued from the excesses and evils of their interest in popular culture," reports media literacy pioneer and Temple University professor Renee Hobbs. Others point out that the protectionist approach "privileges" certain texts over others, and substitutes value judgments for truly critical analyses.

Yet Bob McCannon, head of the New Mexico Media Literacy Project, asserts that it is "a myth that 'protectionist' media literacy does not work. On the contrary, when people are inspired to analyze their hypermediated culture and live a life for themselves and not Coke, Mastercharge, Budweiser, consumerism, fashion ads, Big Media, Big Tobacco and the corporate hegemony, it is the most powerful motivator for kids and citizens."

More than a Vaccine

Media literacy is admittedly "more than a vaccine," McCannon says; very few successful programs "are just bashing and protecting." On the contrary, they "respect kids' views, encourage questioning, and value popular media." But they also criticize mass media producers when they deserve it. Marieli Rowe of the National Telemedia Council replies that McCannon's approach "has powerful popular appeal but it does not educate young people to acquire the ability for autonomous critical thinking. Instead, it successfully indoctrinates them to accept preconceived value judgments."

The tension between simple protectionism and more nuanced understanding of media's influence will continue, if only because the protectionist approach is directly responsive to concerns about media violence, drugs, and other subjects, and thus more likely to receive government funding and popular support. One of the challenges for media literacy education, then, is to build public support for approaches that go beyond simple protectionism and teach youngsters to adopt an overall more critical stance toward the dizzying variety of popular culture available to them.

In this scenario, media literacy is an important response to a media-saturated society but is more than simply a vaccine against sexual risk-taking, gender stereotypes, or violence on TV. In much the same way that analyzing *The Canterbury Tales* might lead students to discover how Chaucer used poetry to make a statement about medieval ideas of morality or class, media literacy education can teach students about the subtle ways their own world is presented to them. In the process, it can not only relieve pressures for government censorship, but empower youth to defend their own free expression rights.

A Parent Advocates Engaging Children About Media Indecency

Barry Fagin

Barry Fagin is a professor of computer science at the U.S. Air Force Academy, a senior fellow in technology policy at the Independence Institute, and a founder of Families Against Internet Censorship. In the following personal account, Fagin describes why, as a parent, he does not advocate censorship or rating schemes in response to indecency in the media. Instead, writes Fagin, it is his parental responsibility to not only monitor his own children's media consumption, but also educate them to be responsible consumers. According to Fagin, even some of the more provocative elements in today's mass media—a rap music star's lyrics, for example, which he finds "vile," "shocking," and "profane"—can be used to engage children in thoughtful dialogue about the excesses of modern popular culture.

Colorado has often been said to be a major battleground in the culture wars. If the past two weeks are any indication, I'd have to agree. Shock rocker Marilyn Manson's visit to Denver got the "free speech" versus "protect the children" going at each other, and in my home town of Colorado Springs, a radio station drew national attention when it was fined by the FCC [Federal Communications Commission] for playing a song by [rap music performer] Eminem. As a parent with an interest in civil liberties and a diehard rock fan, I've been following these issues closely.

Make no mistake, Eminem is not for the squeamish. He is vulgar, shocking, profane, and deliberately provocative. He makes fun of those who idolize him, and seems to have contempt for anyone who'd actually buy one of his albums. His lyrics are misogynistic, his riffs are as thin as water, and musically he's completely forgettable. It's hard for me to find anything redeeming in his work.

That's why, as a parent, I can sympathize with the mother who complained to the FCC when she heard Eminem's "The Real Slim

Shady". Even the radio edit version is pretty vile. It's hard enough being a parent these days without having to deal with your kids' exposure to songs about cannibalism, graphic sexuality, and bestiality. That's why the vision of government as a helper in the daunting task of parenting is so seductive. When it comes to parenting, we all could use a little help now and then.

No Legal Restrictions

But it's a vision parents everywhere should resist. Parents should not be enthusiastic about giving up any part of their role as primary caretakers of their children. For make no mistake, when you assume that the Federal Communications Commission's job is to make sure your kids don't hear bad words on the radio, you are falling down on the job as a parent. In my opinion, parents are much better off in a world where there are no legal restrictions on what radio stations can play. That way, all of us will have to engage our kids at an early age to discuss what is out there and why.

That's what I do with my children, and you know what? It works pretty well. My kids are 13 and 11, and my wife and I make sure they're well versed in the excesses of modern popular culture. This has two advantages. By exposing them to some of pop culture's more radical efforts in an environment free from anger and fear, it takes away the "forbidden fruit" syndrome that attracts many teenagers to otherwise unremarkable cultural artifacts. Better still, carefully exposing children to the negative elements of a dynamic capitalist society helps them better appreciate the positive ones. My son, for example, hates "The Real Slim Shady", but loves *Mystery Science Theater*. And why shouldn't he? One is garbage, while the other is terrific.

While we're on the subject of what we can and can't hear, must we have the FCC tell us what we can and can't see? Why can't television content be left to people to decide for themselves? No one has to watch TV (our family doesn't), and content providers can't make money by making shows that alienate their audience. What exactly are we afraid of? There is every reason to assume that if parents know they're the sole source of control over what their children watch, they'll take a much more active role in scrutinizing their children's TV watching.

Nor should movies be let off the hook. The entire movie rating system is silly and pointless, rendered obsolete by technology. When a new film comes out that we might want to see on a family movie night, my wife and I ignore the ratings and go straight to the Internet. Sites like www.kidsinmind.com let us know in excruciating detail what's going to happen before we walk into the theater. As an added bonus, that can help get a good family discussion going about what writers put into movies, and why.

In my own personal journey through politics and parenting, I've become convinced that content-based regulations in any medium accomplish nothing more than making their advocates feel good about themselves. Most parents, including myself, would rather raise children than fight political battles, but I think it's an issue we ignore at our peril. Raising moral, responsible children is simply too important a task to entrust to anyone else.

A PROFESSOR IS FIRED FOR GIVING VOICE TO HIS POLITICAL DISSENT

Sami Al-Arian

The following personal account was written by former University of South Florida professor Sami Al-Arian, whose views in support of militant Islamic groups thrust him into the center of a raging controversy over the limits of free expression and its relation to academia. In December 2001, Al-Arian, a tenured professor, was fired after pro-Palestinian statements he made years earlier were cast into the public spotlight. As Al-Arian recounts the events that led to his termination, he describes why he remains deeply committed to the principle of free speech. To Al-Arian, even unpopular speech is constitutionally protected; silencing individuals who express dissenting political views erodes the very foundations of democracy. Al-Arian is currently the president of the National Coalition to Protect Political Freedom.

It wasn't quite 9:30 yet on the morning of this dreadful Tuesday [September 11, 2001] when someone approached me as I was speaking to a few students at a local Islamic school. He asked, "Did you hear about what happened in New York?" As we rushed to the nearest TV, our hearts sank as we saw horrifying scenes of planes crashing into buildings and people running for safety. Everyone in the room became suddenly speechless. Soon our shock turned to sadness, then to anger. Some were sobbing. It was an agonizing and solemn moment.

Soon after the media descended on our Islamic center, and before we realized it, we became part of the news. We expressed our deep sorrow and grief. We condemned this criminal act and supported the government in its call for justice against the perpetrators and their benefactors. We joined our fellow citizens in prayer services in many churches starting on the evening of that dark Tuesday.

On Wednesday—the day after the tragedy—seventy-five members of our mosque donated blood. We felt patriotic, but more importantly, part of a national mobilization for doing good. In addition, over $10,000 was collected for the victims' fund of the Red Cross. On Friday, I gave a sermon in the mosque conveying the Islamic teachings in the Qur'an and from the prophet's life that totally reject the logic of indiscriminate killing and hatred. *"Whoever kills one innocent life is as though he killed the whole humanity, and whoever saves one life is as though he saved the whole of humanity,"* the Qur'an teaches. I further reiterated the Islamic principles of cooperation, unity, and tolerance for all faith communities. Needless to say, in all of our interviews with the media, we expressed our heartfelt grief, sadness, and condemnation.

By the following Sunday our call to an ecumenical service in our mosque the previous day in a full-page advertisement brought over four hundred people—more than half non-Muslims. The service was beautiful. All three Abrahamic faiths were represented. We were united in our grief as well as in our determination to overcome this tragedy. I explained in this almost three-hour service how Islam not only condemned this crime but also called for justice. We said that whoever did this evil act could not invoke religion or use religious texts to justify their twisted logic.

While we were engaging in all of that, our community was suffering from the backlash of misguided people and some media outlets. A gun was fired at a mosque in the area. Several members were harassed with ugly words and acts. Women with their traditional Muslim scarves were especially easy targets for hate-filled comments and gestures. Arab-looking people were taken off airplanes. Others were fired from their jobs. The nonstop talk shows on the radio and television continued to attack the Islamic faith to the point that even some children questioned their parents about why they were Muslim. We had to heighten security at our mosque and school to the tune of $20,000. We felt it was unfair that the Arab and Muslim communities not only had to suffer because of the tragedy at the hands of the terrorists, but they also had to endure the hate, distrust, and threats from their fellow citizens. It must be said on the other hand, however, that we received as a community, as well as personally, many heartfelt expressions of love, support, and embrace. They represented the best of America. We made many new friends.

The Fox Network Interview

But the sense of inclusion would soon disappear. On Wednesday, September 26, almost two weeks after the tragedy, I was called by one of the producers of the *O'Reilly Factor* of the Fox News Network. She asked me if I would be a guest on the show and primarily explain the relationship between a think tank I co-founded called World and Islam Studies Enterprise (WISE), established in 1990 and closed in 1995, and the University of South Florida (USF); what the purpose of WISE was; and the controversy that surrounded it six years ago. After much discussion it was agreed that because of the limited time, the show would only address WISE's relationship with USF. I also told her that although I was on the faculty of USF, I wanted to be introduced as chairman of the coalition that was established to defend civil rights and political freedom. Unfortunately, this was never mentioned, because clearly the intent was to put pressure on the university.

Needless to say, the interview was anything but what it was purported to be. The host turned it into a guilt-by-association exercise. You knew A, B, and C. A, B, and C are bad people, therefore you are bad, and must be marked. This was yellow journalism and McCarthyism at its worst. Not only did the producers lie about the purpose of the interview, but also most of what the host said was old news, inaccurate, irrelevant, bigoted, and, most importantly, lacked time-frame and context. On their printed version they called the show "Professor or Terrorist?"

Three individuals were mentioned during this brief "interview." The first topic was a seven-year-old situation that resulted in an extensive investigation by the government, as well as an investigation by USF conducted in 1996 by the former president of the America Bar Association, William Reece Smith, Jr. No wrongdoing was ever found. And certainly no charges were ever filed as a result of these investigations. Mr. O'Reilly never mentioned the time frame of this situation, and that it had absolutely nothing to do with the September 11 tragedy.

Another individual that was mentioned was Dr. Mazen al-Najjar, who is also my brother-in-law. He was never charged or implicated in any wrongdoing. A judge ruled in October 2000 that there was absolutely no evidence that he did anything wrong, and that he was not a threat to national security. Judge R. Kevin McHugh said in his ruling: "Although there were allegations that the ICP [another charity] and WISE were fronts for Palestinian political causes, there is no evidence before the Court that demonstrates that either organization was a front for the P[alestinian] I[slamic] J[ihad]. To the contrary, there is evidence in the record to support the conclusion that WISE was a reputable and scholarly research center and the ICP was highly regarded."

It was simply irresponsible journalism for some media outlets to exploit the current tragedy and deflect the blame, looking for scapegoats so that they might increase ratings or serve their hidden agenda. After the program aired on the Fox news channel, I received death threats as well as numerous hate-filled emails. It was terrorism perpetrated by journalists against innocent civilians and public institutions. Because of these threats against me and the university, USF administrators put me on paid leave because of their "concern" about my safety and the safety of USF. I regretted the decision because over ninety of my students were affected by it. I was also disappointed that the administration did not forcefully defend academic freedom.

After the Fox network interview, many other media outlets started their own onslaught and attacks on me because of anti-Israeli positions or statements I made many years ago. For instance, as I was active during the first Palestinian uprising (intifada) between 1987 and 1993, the words "death to Israel" were uttered in one of the rallies in 1988. The reference to this slogan spoken fourteen years ago was in the context of a speech, given in Arabic, about the brutal and continuing occupation of the Palestinians by Israel. It simply meant death to occupation, to oppression, to the Israeli apartheid system instituted against the Palestinians. It certainly did not mean death to any Jewish person, as it was being portrayed. In this I am reminded of the early American revolutionary patriots such as Patrick Henry, Joseph Warren, and the poet John Trumbull. They called for the "burial of the British Empire," and wished for the "Empire's everlasting grave." I'm sure that these early American patriots did not mean to bury the citizens of the British Empire, but rather to end the brutal British occupation of America. Patrick Henry's "Give me liberty or give me death" speech during the American Revolution is probably one of the most admired speeches of all time. His words describing the American sentiments against the British then prophetically tell of the Palestinians' plight and their predicament today.

Termination

Nevertheless, the media attacks as well as an orchestrated campaign that was waged by pro-Zionist groups across the U.S. continued to pressure the university to terminate my employment, although I have been at the university since 1986. On December 19, 2001, the USF Board of Trustees met in an "emergency" meeting and recommended my termination. Later that day, USF president Judy Genshaft sent me a notice of her intention to terminate my employment despite the fact that I have been tenured for ten years.

During all my USF years my record shows that I have always conducted myself professionally. I love the teaching profession and have always enjoyed the challenges of the classroom. I received the best-teacher award as well as the prestigious Teaching Incentive Award in the College of Engineering. I have over forty publications, including a chapter that just appeared in the Mechatronics handbook in early 2002.

The USF president gave three frivolous reasons for terminating my employment at a public institution. First, she maintained that I did not make it clear when I appeared on the Fox news program that I was not speaking on behalf of the university. Secondly, that I appeared on campus once in early October. And finally, she claimed that I caused disruption at the university because of the death threats against me, the hate mail that ensued, and supposedly the decline in financial contributions to the university and its alumni association.

Needless to say, I was invited on that program not because I was a USF faculty member, but because I was considered a leader in the American Muslim community, as well as a civil rights activist. Obviously, I do not speak, nor have I ever spoken, on behalf of the univer-

sity. I have on many occasions made it clear to journalists and reporters that I speak as a leader of the American Muslim and Arab community and in my capacity as the president of the National Coalition
to Protect Political Freedom (NCPPF), a group of over forty organizations coming together to defend civil and constitutional rights. A July
16, 2001, article in *Newsweek* magazine about the participation of
Arab-Americans in the 2000 campaign reported: "Al-Arian is one of
the country's leading advocates for repeal of secret-evidence laws." I
was not identified in that article as a USF professor, but as the country's leading advocate in an important civil rights issue.

Furthermore, I came once to campus on October 5, 2001, to address
a campus student organization that I advise. If I had thought that I was
"banned" from coming to campus I certainly would not have attended.
In fact, the USF provost told me that I could meet with my graduate
students on nights and weekends during our conversation on September 27, 2001, when he placed me on paid leave for "safety." When the
police asked me if everything was all right on the day I talked to my
students, they did not ask me to leave because they did not know that
the purported ban was in effect. As for the disruption, it's a classic
"blame the victim" argument that defies logic and rationality.

Academic Free Speech

I was eighteen when I took my first civics course during my sopho-
more year, in 1976. On the first day of class, the professor talked
about the two Ds of American government, as he called them: due
process and dissent. Ironically, a quarter of a century later, these two
important concepts are at the center of my professional career. I was
neither afforded any due process, nor was my right of political dissent
respected or penalty-free as promised by the Constitution. This case is
indeed about academic freedom and freedom of speech.

I did not choose to be the poster child for the debate about academic freedom in the post–September 11 world. Now that I am, however, some important questions in this debate must be raised and dis-
cussed by all academics:

- Are university administrators justified in terminating the employment of a sixteen-year-tenured faculty member because he
  did not accompany off-campus remarks with a disclaimer that he
  wasn't speaking on behalf of the university?
- Should university administrators be able to fire a tenured faculty
  member because he attended a meeting on campus while on paid
  leave?
- Should university administrators be allowed to dismiss a tenured
  faculty member because his public pronouncements conflict
  with the political views of those in power?

Indeed, if the termination is allowed to stand, then all faculty across
the nation will be vulnerable as to their job security and the profes-

sional compromises they may be required to make to keep their jobs.

As someone who has lived in the U.S. for over a quarter-century, I value our freedom and openness. I believe the Islamic faith, which has been vilified in post–September 11 America, is not only compatible with democracy, but cannot be fully practiced without it. I believe in the American political system and in the Constitution. If I disagree with a governmental policy, I believe in working within the system to improve it. And this is what I have practiced and taught my children. For over four years, my wife and I have visited over 150 congressional offices in order to ban the use of secret evidence. I believe that we were very effective in bringing to the attention of many members of Congress the due process concerns associated with the use of secret evidence. I believe that our hard work paid off when President [George W.] Bush and many political leaders spoke against it during the 2000 political campaigns.

Many people have pleaded with me to simply remain silent. This is exactly what my critics want. Some think that there are powerful groups that are out to get me. My answer is simple. I believe in freedom of speech now more than ever. I believe that people have the right to hear what some may consider "unpopular" views as much as I have the obligation to express my beliefs and opinions.

CHAPTER 5

CIVIL LIBERTIES IN THE AGE OF TERRORISM

THE TENSION BETWEEN CIVIL LIBERTIES AND NATIONAL SECURITY

Jerel A. Rosati

Jerel A. Rosati is a professor of political science and international studies at the University of South Carolina. According to Rosati, the terrorist attacks on September 11, 2001, and the consequent war on terror clearly demonstrate the tension between the contradictory demands of national security and the preservation of personal freedoms. To fully understand the nation's struggle to persist as an open society in the wake of September 11, Rosati writes, the war on terror must not be viewed in isolation, but rather placed in historical perspective. Rosati observes that the government has indeed curtailed civil liberties during past periods of national crisis. By the same token, Americans are less willing, perhaps, to sacrifice their civil liberties during times of peace. Whether the current war on terror will result in a far-reaching abridgement of personal liberties, according to Rosati, has yet to be determined.

The September 11 tragedy and the War on Terror have clearly demonstrated the tension between the demands of national security and the demands of democracy in the making of U.S. foreign policy. Democracy requires an open political process and high levels of civil rights and liberties in order for its citizens to politically participate. The demands of national security usually require a much less open political process with limitations on civil rights and liberties. The demands of democracy and the demands of national security inherently have contradictory implications for political participation within a democratic society. . . .

The Preoccupation with National Security Versus Democratic Liberties

Under conditions of war, American civil liberties and political participation are often curtailed and violated in a systematic way by the govern-

Jerel A. Rosati, "At Odds with One Another: The Tension Between Civil Liberties and National Security in Twentieth-Century America," in *American National Security and Civil Liberties in an Era of Terrorism,* edited by David B. Cohen and John W. Wells. New York: Palgrave Macmillan, 2004. Copyright © 2004 by David B. Cohen and John W. Wells. All rights reserved. Reproduced by permission of the publisher.

ment, usually with the active support of groups and people throughout society. This typically occurs because the demands of national security take precedence over the demands of democracy during war, where most segments of society tend to rally behind the president and the government in order to fight the enemy abroad. It is in the context of this political environment that the government's and, in particular, the president's ability to dominate the politics of U.S. foreign policy is maximized. This is because wars and national emergencies, in particular, tend to be times when little tolerance exists for individuals and groups that politically criticize or challenge the government's foreign policy or the status quo within society.

The general American tendency toward conformity, as stated by political scientist Seymour Martin Lipset, "has been noted as a major aspect of American culture from [Alexis de] Tocqueville in the 1830s to [David] Riesman [in *The Lonely Crowd*] in the 1950s." In fact, times of perceived threats to national security are often accompanied by what historian Richard Hofstadter has called "the paranoid style in American politics." In other words, war often produces a preoccupation with internal threats to national security, and certain groups within society are targeted as security risks because of their ethnicity or political beliefs.

The net result is that the ability to politically participate and exercise civil liberties tends to be limited during periods of conflict because the government's war effort, combined with American nationalism and superpatriotism, tolerates little dissent and encourages political repression. Witness, for example, the furor surrounding the country band the Dixie Chicks when in March 2003, on the eve of the Iraq War, lead singer Natalie Maines told her London concertgoers that "we're ashamed the president of the United States is from Texas." The remark was followed by scores of radio stations boycotting their music as well as publicity events in which their albums were destroyed. The band later apologized for the comment after being pressured by their recording label. This episode represents the "underside" of American history that is too often ignored, yet it has been part of American history and is important to know in order to understand the evolution of political participation and the politics of U.S. foreign policy.

There have been three major periods in the twentieth century when the demands of national security have prevailed over the demands of democracy and the exercise of civil liberties in domestic politics has been severely curtailed: 1) World War I; 2) World War II; and 3) the cold war. Each of these periods has been accompanied by the supremacy of the president in the making of U.S. foreign policy.

The years after the Vietnam War, however, have been characterized by a decline in the demands of national security throughout American society, creating an uneasy tension between national security and democracy. This development has led to a corresponding rise in the liberty of Americans to fully exercise their civil rights in electoral and group politics in order to influence the future of U.S. foreign policy. The net result is that presidents have had to operate in a political environment where they have had greater difficulty exercising power in the politics of U.S. foreign policy. The terrorist attacks of September 11, 2001, and the war on terrorism may have again altered the tense dynamics between the demands of national security and democracy and its corresponding implications for exercising presidential power in foreign policy at the beginning of the twenty-first century despite the collapse of the cold war. . . .

The threat to civil liberties during this new war on terrorism is no doubt great. Whether or not the war on terrorism will be a sustained long-term conflict resulting in a permanent crackdown on individual liberties and expression has yet to be determined. Ultimately, much will depend on how the following questions are eventually addressed by the American political process: *Will the [George W.] Bush administration's war on terrorism resonate in the long run within the domestic political environment and especially among the American people? Will Americans feel it's a time of war and national emergency?* If so, the result will likely be greater presidential power and greater ability to exercise prerogative government in the name of national security. Or, *will Americans feel that it is "war in a time of peace," with diminishing fears and concerns about the threat of terrorism?* If so, the chances increase that the demands of democracy will resurface, making violations of civil rights and liberties more politically controversial and damaging.

The answers are unclear; the future remains uncertain. Much will depend on events and reactions, especially concerning the frequency and intensity of future terrorist attacks by foreigners on Americans and on American soil. Such uncertainty means that there will be an uneasy, and changing, tension and balance between the demands of national security and the demands of democracy. The future of civil rights and liberties of many people hang in the balance.

THE PATRIOT ACT CURTAILS CIVIL LIBERTIES

Julian Sanchez

Since its passage following the September 11, 2001, attacks, the USA Patriot Act has significantly broadened the powers of domestic law enforcement and international intelligence agencies in the interest of thwarting future terrorist attacks. Julian Sanchez is among those who view the Patriot Act as a brazen violation of the country's most cherished civil liberties—equality before the law and restraints on the exercise of police powers, for instance. To support his view, Sanchez refutes several popular defenses of the Patriot Act—that the magnitude of the terrorist threat justifies expanded governmental power, for example, or that an adequate system of checks and balances prevents egregious civil liberties violations. Sanchez is an assistant editor at *Reason*.

It's official: The fashionable fall meme [contagious idea] for unreconstructed [George W.] Bush administration cheerleaders is the notion that civil-libertarian concerns about the PATRIOT Act have been much ado about nothing: the squawking of so many Chicken Littles.

The defense of PATRIOT has been slow in coming, in part because it was possible, at first, to dismiss criticism as predictable carping from the usual suspects: the American Civil Liberties Union [ACLU], the Electronic Frontier Foundation, and other notorious "fifth columnists," to borrow the new right's sledgehammer-subtle imprecation *du jour*. Things became trickier once American Baptist Churches, the American Conservative Union, Gun Owners of America, and folks like Georgia ex-representative Bob Barr began voicing reservations. The conservative base has begun to get nervous.

The most widely cited Chicken Little piece so far is an article in the Summer issue of *City Journal* by Manhattan Institute scholar Heather Mac Donald, who has presumably shifted her attention away from stumping for Total-cum-Terrorism Information Awareness now that even the Republican controlled Senate has backed away from the proposal to create a national data panopticon. Abbreviated follow-up defenses—mostly Cliffs Notes to Mac Donald's argument—have since issued from the pens of the *Washington Times'* editors and, most recently, *National Review's* Rich Lowry.

In the Name of War

Each piece trots out the "don't you realize we're at war?" trope, which it's tempting to read as an imputation to civil libertarians of almost mindboggling naiveté. They are not (as one might think) animated by a concern that liberties may be sacrificed without any appreciable gain in security, or an insistence that law enforcement show that existing powers have been used effectively—a highly dubious proposition—before expansive new powers are granted. No, the ACLU and company have apparently just been snoozing for two years: They missed the news about that little dust-up involving a couple of planes and skyscrapers two Septembers ago.

In reality, though, civil liberties groups may well be unaware that we're "at war" in the sense that Mac Donald intends the phrase. She avers, for example, that the detention of executive-designated "enemy combatants" is "fully justified under the laws of war." She means, in short, that all the powers a government might exercise during a conventional military war, say World War II, are equally appropriate in the War on Terror. Since "terror" is a notoriously nebulous enemy—it is, after all, an abstraction, not a country—and the conditions of victory uncertain, this amounts, if we take it literally, to a functionally indefinite arrogation of "emergency" powers to the executive.

Oddly, this sweeping claim of authority is typically coupled with the insistence that PATRIOT has given us nothing (or nothing much) new under the sun. PATRIOT apologists point out, for example, that grand juries have long been able to subpoena the sorts of records—including, potentially sensitive financial documents, the membership rosters of religious or political organizations, and lists of books checked out from local libraries—now available to federal investigators. Tim Lynch, director of the Cato Institute's Project on Criminal Justice and co-author of the study "A Grand Façade: How the Grand Jury Was Captured by Government", argues that this reasoning gets things backwards. "The grand juries are already out of control," Lynch says, "and now they're saying 'let's build on that'?"

Grand juries, after all, were initially intended as a check on prosecutorial power, a means of verifying that solid evidence existed to justify an indictment. It may be that they have, over time, become an extension of prosecutorial power, but it's not clear that this one means of circumventing the Fourth Amendment should be allowed to metastasize. The situations are not entirely analogous either: Unlike grand jury subpoenas, those allowed under PATRIOT's Section 215 come with gag orders attached. Those served with demands for records are unable to make the public aware of those demands or to challenge them in court. Grand jury subpoenas for potentially sensitive materials are at least subject to challenge on First or Fourth Amendment grounds.

Lowry and others are quick to point out that judicial review is not *entirely* absent from the process:

> The fact is that federal authorities cannot do any of the nasty things under the Patriot Act that critics complain about—electronic surveillance, record searches, etc.—without a court order and a showing of probable cause. A federal judge has to sign off on any alleged "violation of civil liberties."

This would be welcome news—if it were true. Alas, Lowry is here mistaken, incorrect, uttering un-facts, speaking that-which-is-not. Law enforcement agents need not show probable cause, nor were they required to do so when exercising the equivalent powers under the Foreign Intelligence Surveillance Act of 1978 [FISA]. The difference is that whereas previously, authorities were required to adduce some "reason to believe"—a lower standard than "probable cause"—that the target of investigation was an agent of a foreign power (including a terrorist group), it now need only claim that records are "sought in connection with" a terrorist investigation, with no requirement of particularized suspicion.

But what of that precious judicial oversight? Are PATRIOT critics trying, as Mac Donald alleges, to "hide the judge," who presumably can be relied upon to check abuse of these new powers?

It would be more accurate to say that apologists are hiding behind the judge. FISA courts have rejected precisely one federal wiretap or subpoena request in the course of 25 years. Worse, the text of the Patriot Act stipulates that judges "shall issue" warrants, provided that the request certifies that the records specified are sought in connection with a terror investigation. This is neither a "check" nor a "balance": It is a tricycle-sized speed bump placed in the path of an Abrams Tank.

Other Misleading Claims

Equally misleading is the claim that the authorization of "roving wiretaps" represents nothing more than the natural extension to terrorism cases of a power that already exists for domestic organized crime investigations. This is a red herring: Civil liberties advocates do not argue that roving taps are inappropriate to terrorism investigations. They do note, however, that the roving tap authority was quite deliberately *not limited* to such cases: Federal authorities insisted on having comparable powers for drug trafficking or tax evasion inquiries. The drug and terror wars may now be fused still further by the Vital Interdiction of Criminal Terrorist Organizations Act, which has been dubbed the "VICTORY Act," despite the failure of the drafters to come up with a final two words to complete the acronym. Perhaps the meanings of the "R" and "Y" are classified. [The Victory Act was never submitted to Congress.]

As Jim Dempsey of the Center for Democracy and Technology noted at an April forum sponsored by Cato, amendments to the roving wiretap authority in the Intelligence Authorization Act may broaden its effect still further. Warrants may now rove, not only over places and telephones, but over persons as well. The government, in short, may request a blanket order covering an "unknown person at an unknown location."

Debate over these particulars, however, is probably secondary. Most troubling is the lax standard some conservatives now seem to have adopted for evaluating expansions of government power. According to Lowry, "The challenge to critics should be this: Name one civil liberty that has been violated under the Patriot Act." One might, at least arguably, cite news that the FBI had sought and obtained the records of several million students at SCUBA schools as evidence of a troubling fishing-expedition approach, but it's true that there are few clear cases of overreach at which PATRIOT critics can point.

Legislation Shrouded in Secrecy

Of course, that's roughly what one should expect from a law distinguished by the amount of secrecy it imposes. Lowry's demand amounts to: "Show me just one classified, top-secret abuse of power!" As such, the request is disingenuous at the very least. The American Civil Liberties Union (ACLU) filed a Freedom of Information Act request for information on the uses of PATRIOT powers last August 2002, and was rebuffed. "It is literally impossible," observes ACLU staff attorney Jameel Jaffer, "to know in what contexts the government has used these powers unless they tell us of their own accord, which they have so far refused to do."

Even if we assume officials have thus far been positively angelic in their use of PATRIOT powers, there is something disconcerting about this line of attack. The argument that there's nothing to fear because we have not, in the two years since PATRIOT's hasty passage, seen egregious civil liberties violations is a warped bit of inductive logic on par with concluding that Russian roulette is safe because the chamber's clicked twice. It used to be a distinctive conservative virtue to focus on the institutional tendencies created by a law, rather than taking comfort because it's good ol' John Ashcroft rather than Janet Reno at the helm [of the office of the U.S. Attorney General].

The Burden of Proof

The broadest thing wrong with this standard, though, is where it places the burden of proof. Civil libertarians want the answer to questions that as yet have barely been asked and never been answered: How will these new powers make us safer? Would they have prevented the September 11 attacks? Do they add anything to the existing powers the government failed to deploy effectively before then? Are they broader than necessary to aid in the fight against terror?

The PATRIOT apologists will have none of this. The default, as they see it, is to grant new powers unless there's proof that they'll lead overnight to tyranny. The presumption of liberty is replaced by a presumption of power. The sad reality, though, is that even a police state can't guarantee total safety: Whatever we do, the coming years will see more terror, more attacks. If we conclude, each time, that the culprit must be an excess of domestic freedom, a lack of government power, we are traveling a road with no end.

ANTI-TERROR INITIATIVES DO NOT DIMINISH CIVIL LIBERTIES

Rich Lowry

According to Rich Lowry, the enactment of the Patriot Act has not unduly suppressed civil liberties. Rather, the majority of legal changes after the terrorist attacks of September 11, 2001, simply updated existing laws to give counterterrorism investigators the same powers investigators already have in other criminal justice areas—organized crime cases, for example. As before, existing judicial and statutory safeguards continue to protect the rights of citizens. These anti-terror measures, Lowry maintains, have made Americans safer; it is absolutely imperative, then, that the government remain well equipped to deal with conditions that threaten the nation's well-being. Lowry is an editor of *National Review* and the author of *Legacy: Paying the Price for the Clinton Years.*

The war on terror has finally, as some critics always warned it would, whipped up a dangerous hysteria. It just so happens that the hysteria has taken hold among critics of the war on terror. They argue that the USA Patriot Act is a combination of the Alien and Sedition Acts [measures taken during World War I to deport foreigners suspected of espionage or imprison anyone suspected of seditious behavior] and Kristallnacht [a Nazi terror campaign against German Jews], in a smear campaign that threatens to roll back policies that have made Americans safer after Sept. 11.

The campaign includes over-the-top editorial writers (the *Cleveland Plain Dealer* calls the act "the seed stock of a police state"), raving civil libertarians (American Civil Liberties Union [ACLU]: "a disturbing power") and chest-beating presidential candidates (Howard Dean: erodes "the rights of average Americans"). According to Wisconsin's Democratic Sen. Russ Feingold, you should sell your stock in Amazon.com—the Patriot Act has made Americans "afraid to read books."

The challenge to critics should be this: Name one civil liberty that has been violated under the Patriot Act. They can't, which is why they instead rely on hyperbole in an increasingly successful effort to make the Patriot Act a dirty phrase.

Rich Lowry, "Patriot Hysteria: The Zacarias Moussaoui Protection Act," *National Review Online,* August 28, 2003. Copyright © 2003 by King Features Syndicate. Reproduced by permission.

Powers That Already Exist

Many of the new powers under the act—such as "the roving wiretap," which allows the government to continue monitoring a target who switches phones—aren't really new. They give counterterrorism investigators the same powers investigators already have in mob cases. Opponents of the act must explain why Mohammad Atta [one of the September 11 hijackers] should have greater freedom from surveillance than Tony Soprano [a mobster character from the popular HBO program *The Sopranos*].

The fact is that federal authorities cannot do any of the nasty things under the Patriot Act that critics complain about—electronic surveillance, record searches, etc.—without a court order and a showing of probable cause. A federal judge has to sign off on any alleged "violation of civil liberties."

Two particular provisions of the act rile critics. The Republican-controlled House—demonstrating that uninformed hysteria is bipartisan—recently voted to ban funding for Section 213 of the law. Under Section 213, law enforcement can delay notifying a target that his property has been searched. These delayed-notification searches require a court order, and they can be used only when immediate notification would jeopardize an investigation.

Such searches already existed prior to the passage of the Patriot Act, and the Supreme Court has upheld their constitutionality. Federal counterterrorism investigators have asked for delayed searches roughly 50 times during the past two years, and the average delay in notification has been about a week—hardly totalitarianism.

Another target of critics is Section 215. It allows investigators to seize documents—including, theoretically, library records—from a third party if they bear on a terrorism investigation. The ACLU says that this means the FBI has the power to "spy on a person because they don't like the book she reads." But this is another power that already existed. Grand juries have always been able to subpoena records if they are relevant to a criminal investigation. The Patriot Act extends this power to counterterrorism investigators and requires a court order for it to be used.

Critics want to eviscerate these sections of the act, and more. They should bundle their proposals together and call them "The Zacarias Moussaoui Protection Act," after "the 20th hijacker," whose computer wasn't searched prior to Sept. 11 due to civil-liberties concerns. We have already forgotten the importance of aggressive, pre-emptive law enforcement. The locus of forgetfulness is the Democratic presidential field, as Rep. Dick Gephardt, Sen. John Edwards and Sen. John Kerry all voted for the Patriot Act and now attack Attorney General John Ashcroft [Alberto Gonzalez replaced Ashcroft as attorney general in February 2005] for having the temerity to use it.

Out on the Democratic hustings, it's as if Sept. 11 never happened. Of course, no organization contributed so much to the lax law enforcement that made possible the murder of 3,000 Americans that day than the ACLU. Mohammed Atta and Co. should have remembered it in their prayers as they screamed toward their targets. If the ACLU gets its way on the Patriot Act, some future successful terrorists will want to remember it in their prayers as well.

THE RIGHTS OF UNLAWFUL ENEMY COMBATANTS SHOULD BE RESTRICTED

Robert H. Bork

On November 13, 2001, President George W. Bush, citing the "extraordinary emergency" created by the September 11, 2001, terrorist attacks, signed an executive order allowing the use of military tribunals to try non-U.S. citizens accused of terrorism. The November 13 order and similar laws and regulations that pertain to unlawful enemy combatants—including U.S. citizens—have been the subject of intense controversy. In the following viewpoint, Robert H. Bork counters claims that the Bush administration has flagrantly violated many constitutional safeguards for the accused. Drawing on the cases of Zacarias Moussaoui and other high-profile enemies who are not fighting as lawful combatants (as the United States defines them), Bork argues that the rights of due process—access to legal counsel, for example—do not apply to enemies engaged in terrorism or other unlawful conflict against Americans. Bork is a fellow at the American Enterprise Institute for Public Policy Research. He has served as solicitor general of the United States, as well as a U.S. Court of Appeals judge.

According to critics, by depriving certain captured individuals of access to lawyers, and by holding them without filing charges, the government is violating the Geneva Convention's protections of lawful combatants or prisoners of war. This is nonsense.

Treatment of Captured Terrorists

Four criteria must be met to qualify a person as a lawful combatant. He must be under the command of a person responsible for his subordinates; wear a fixed distinctive emblem recognizable at a distance; carry arms openly; and conduct operations in accordance with the laws and customs of war. The men the United States has captured and detained so far do not meet these criteria.

The government's policy is as follows: if a captured unlawful enemy combatant is believed to have further information about terrorism, he can be held without access to legal counsel and without charges being filed. Once the government is satisfied that it has all the relevant information it can obtain, the captive can be held until the end of hostilities, or be released, or be brought up on charges before a criminal court.

The government chose one of these options when it charged John Lindh, an American citizen who fought with the Taliban in Afghanistan, and Zacarias Moussaoui, who is thought to have been involved in the planning for September 11, with crimes. Lindh entered into a plea agreement under which he was sentenced to twenty years in prison. Moussaoui's case has proved more complicated. The government proposes to use only unclassified materials in its prosecution, but Moussaoui, a French citizen of Moroccan heritage who has admitted in open court to belonging to al Qaeda [the terrorist organization responsible for the 9/11 attacks] and swearing allegiance to Osama bin Laden [the mastermind of those attacks], has demanded to see classified materials and to have access to other captured terrorists for the preparation of his defense.

For obvious reasons, Moussaoui's demands are unacceptable to the government, which does not want to divulge classified information or allow terrorists to communicate with each other. But the prosecutors' offer of an alternative procedure was rejected by the presiding judge. If the government continues to be unsuccessful in its determination to protect classified information, it may decide to prosecute Moussaoui in special military tribunals created for trying terrorists. That would surely trigger the outrage of civil libertarians, even though it is plainly arguable that Moussaoui could and perhaps should have been prosecuted there in the first place. I will return to this issue below.

Detention of U.S. Citizens

In a somewhat separate category from Lindh and Moussaoui, both of whom have been charged with actual crimes, are the cases of two American citizens who have been detained rather than brought to trial because the government believes they possess undivulged valuable information. Yaser Esam Hamdi remains confined to the Norfolk Naval Brig, and Jose Padilla is confined at the Consolidated Naval Brig in Charleston. Neither man has yet been charged.

Hamdi filed a petition for habeas corpus challenging the legality of his detention. Although he was captured in Afghanistan, where he was carrying an AK-47 during a time of active military hostilities, and although he was classified by the executive branch as an unlawful enemy combatant, Hamdi claimed the full protections of the Constitution as an American citizen. He argued that his detention without charge and without access to a judicial tribunal or the right to counsel was in violation of the Fifth and Fourteenth Amendments.

The Court of Appeals for the Fourth Circuit held otherwise. Although the detention of U.S. citizens is subject to judicial review, that review must be "deferential." The Constitution explicitly confers war powers on the political branches; in going to war in Afghanistan, the President had relied both on those powers and on Congress's authorization of "all necessary and appropriate force" against nations, organizations, or persons he determined to be involved in terrorist attacks. Hamdi, the court said, was indeed an enemy combatant subject to detention. It elaborated its rationale:

> The detention of enemy combatants serves at least two vital purposes. First, detention prevents enemy combatants from rejoining the enemy and continuing to fight against America and its allies. . . . In this respect, "captivity is neither a punishment nor an act of vengeance," but rather "a simple war measure."

> Second, detention in lieu of prosecution may relieve the burden on military commanders of litigating the circumstances of a capture halfway around the globe. . . . As the Supreme Court has recognized [in *Johnson v. Eisentrager* (1950)], "it would be difficult to devise more effective fettering of a field commander than to allow the very enemies he is ordered to reduce to submission to call him to account in his own civil courts and divert his efforts and attention from the military offensive abroad to the legal defense at home."

Hamdi's petition was denied, as was his right of access to an attorney or to seeing government documents. [On October 9, 2004, Hamdi was released and deported to Saudi Arabia.]

Padilla was arrested upon his arrival at Chicago's O'Hare airport from Pakistan. The government indicted him, claiming he planned acts of terrorism, including the explosion of a radioactive "dirty bomb." When, like Hamdi, he petitioned for habeas corpus, the court held similarly that "the President is authorized under the Constitution and by law to direct the military to detain enemy combatants." Nevertheless, and over the government's objection, the court said it would allow Padilla the assistance of counsel to litigate the facts surrounding his capture and detention. (The government is now appealing this.) At the same time, the court disallowed the presence of counsel at Padilla's interrogations, and averred that the government need only show "some evidence" to prevail. [On March 1, 2005, a federal judge ruled that the United States cannot hold Padilla without charging him.]

Anthony Lewis went ballistic. It is, he wrote, a "fundamental truth" that an individual cannot get justice against the state without the effective help of a lawyer, and this truth was "being challenged in a way that I did not believe was possible in our country." But Lewis was completely wrong. Despite his attempt to conflate the two categories, detention is not punishment; its purpose, rather, is to prevent members of enemy forces from causing harm while hostilities are in progress. Nor is Padilla the subject of a criminal proceeding; criminal law rules do not apply when detention of an enemy is ordered by the President under his war powers. Hundreds of thousands of lawful prisoners of war have been held by the United States without the right to a lawyer, and unlawful enemy combatants are entitled to even fewer rights.

This makes perfect sense. A judicial system with rights of due process is crucial to a free society, but it is not designed for the protection of enemies engaged in armed conflict against us. Nor can we divert resources from the conduct of a war to the trial of every POW or unlawful combatant who wants to litigate. Besides, giving someone like Padilla a lawyer would frustrate the very purpose of his detention, and place American lives in danger. A lawyer's duty, acting within the bounds of ethical behavior, is to create delay and confusion, keeping alive his client's hopes of going free. Armed with such hopes, Padilla would be all the less likely to divulge what he knew, and plans for future terrorist attacks might thereby go undetected.

It might be argued that Padilla is not like other unlawful enemy combatants because he is a U.S. citizen taken on American soil. But the Supreme Court disposed of that distinction as long ago as 1942 in *parte Quirin*. In that case, German would-be saboteurs had entered the U.S. illegally with the intention of attacking war industries and facilities. Upon capture, they sought habeas corpus, claiming a right to trial before a regular court rather than a military tribunal. In denying the petition, the Court deemed it irrelevant that one of the captives claimed U.S. citizenship and was on U.S. soil when apprehended.

Military Tribunals

This is where there is a role for military tribunals, an institution that has played an important and honorable part in American jurisprudence throughout our history. In *Quirin*, the Court made clear that such tribunals rightly enjoy a separate constitutional track from grand juries and trial by jury, which "at the time of the adoption of the Constitution [were] familiar parts of the machinery for criminal trials in the civil courts." Quite properly, however, the procedures followed by these civil institutions were, and had to be, "unknown to military tribunals[,] which are not courts in the sense of the judiciary articles" of the Constitution.

Consistent with this understanding, military tribunals have been used by several Presidents in time of war. In the Revolutionary War, before there even was a Constitution, George Washington employed them freely. So did Abraham Lincoln in the Civil War, and Franklin D. Roosevelt in World War II. Although we remember the Nuremberg trial, with its many mappings of a civilian court, the victorious Allies did not always regard such open trials as the only or preferred method of proceeding. As the legal scholar Mark Martins reminds us, "German regular army soldiers were also defendants in many of the thousands of military courts and commissions convened by the Allies after the war in different zones of occupation."

In any event, the image of military tribunals as drumhead courts manned by stony-faced officers ready to convict regardless of the evidence is a fantasy. In reality, military courts may achieve just and equitable results more frequently than the run of civilian juries. Military judges tend to be more scrupulous in weighing evidence, in resisting emotional appeals, and in respecting the plain import of the laws. . . . If, as the war against the terrorists drags on, we are forced to have recourse to military tribunals, there may well be clear gains for both justice and security.

There are, to be sure, costs to be paid for going the route of military courts. It was no doubt partly out of a desire to placate critics, both at home and abroad, that President Bush first announced that U.S. citizens would be tried in our regular courts, and that the decision was made to try even Moussaoui in a federal district court, in the future, moreover, some of our allies may refuse to extradite captured terrorists if it is known they are likely to land before a military tribunal.

But the critics show every sign of being implacable, and in any case the cost of staying with the civil route is likely to be higher. In a district court a defense attorney will almost inevitably demand access to classified information; continued disclosure of such information in court would inform not only Muslim terrorists but all the world's intelligence services of the information we have and our methods of gathering it. If compromising national security is one alternative that may be forced on government by the demand for access to classified material, the other is to drop charges. Neither alternative is acceptable.

SAFEGUARDS FOR THE ACCUSED MUST BE PRESERVED

Anthony Lewis

Anthony Lewis was a *New York Times* editorial columnist for thirty-two years and has twice won the Pulitzer Prize for his reporting. Lewis writes that, notwithstanding the magnitude of the September 11, 2001, terrorist attacks, basic constitutional rights for the accused must remain sacrosanct. According to Lewis, these rights, which include habeas corpus, due process of law, right to counsel, and trial by jury, should not be limited to citizens but apply to all individuals subject to U.S. authority. The dangers in relinquishing these rights are profound, writes Lewis; the oppressive treatment of terrorist suspects eviscerates the constitutional safeguards that protect all Americans.

"It is a recurring theme in history that in times of war, armed conflict, or perceived national danger, even liberal democracies adopt measures infringing human rights in ways that are wholly disproportionate to the crisis."
—Lord Johan Steyn, lecture to the British Institute of International and Comparative Law, November 25, 2003

Britain's law lords, who make up the country's highest court, are by tradition a secluded lot, avoiding comments on matters outside of their court. But [in] November [2003] one of them, Lord Steyn, broke those bounds in a dramatic way. He gave a lecture condemning the U.S. government for keeping hundreds of prisoners [both terrorist suspects and Taliban freedom fighters from Afghanistan] in Guantanamo Bay, Cuba, in what he called a "legal black hole"—unable to challenge their imprisonment before any court. Speaking, he said, as a lifelong admirer of American ideals of justice, he called the treatment of the men held at Guantanamo a "monstrous failure of justice."

It is not just for Guantanamo that the alarm bells of American liberty should be sounding. Civil liberties are more broadly in a perilous state, wounded in the historical pattern noted by Lord Steyn: repression in times of perceived national danger. In the name of fighting

Anthony Lewis, "One Liberty at a Time," *Mother Jones,* May/June 2004. Copyright © 2004 by the Foundation for National Progress. Reproduced by permission.

terrorism, President [George W.] Bush and his administration have abruptly overridden rights protected by the Constitution and international law. Ideas foreign to American principles—detention without trial, denial of access to lawyers, years of interrogation in isolation—are now American practices.

A Government Under Law

The danger of what is happening is more profound than the denial of justice to some individuals. The Bush administration is really attacking a basic premise of the American system: that we have a government under law. It was a novel idea when James Madison, Alexander Hamilton, and the rest laid it down at the end of the 18th century, and ever since it has been a distinctive feature of our polity: Political leaders are subject to the law, responsible to legal constraints on their power as well as to the vote of the people. "A government of laws, and not of men," John Adams first said.

The administration's policy, in one instance after another, has been to avoid any accounting before the law. It has tried to prevent the prisoners it holds as possibly connected to terrorism, in Guantanamo and elsewhere, from testing in court whether in fact they have anything to do with terrorism. It has covered its actions in secrecy, which is the enemy of legal and political accountability. Aliens have been the most numerous victims of the administration's methods, but not the only ones. Oppressive tactics used against aliens have been directed against American citizens, too.

In the weeks after September 11, 2001, FBI agents arrested more than 1,000 aliens, most of them Muslims, on suspicion that they might have something to do with terrorism. Many were held for months without charges, in painful conditions. In the words of a *New York Times* legal writer, Adam Liptak, their treatment "inverted the foundation principles of the American legal system."

They were arrested essentially at random, without any probable cause to believe they had terror connections. They were treated as guilty until proved innocent—detained until a lengthy FBI process concluded that they "posed no danger to the United States." Many were held for months after judges ordered them released, or after they had agreed to leave the country because they had overstayed their visas or otherwise violated immigration rules. Some were subjected to abuse in prison, verbal and physical: At the Metropolitan Detention Center in Brooklyn, guards slammed detainees against the wall, hurt them by stepping on their leg chains, kept them in cells with fluorescent lights on 24 hours a day, and told them, "You're going to die here." Of the thousands detained, only two have been charged with a connection to terrorism.

One of the Bush administration's programs that has drawn widespread international criticism is the holding of alleged Taliban fighters and terrorists in prison cages at Guantanamo Bay, Cuba. There are more than 600 prisoners. The general impression is that they were almost all captured by U.S. forces during the war in Afghanistan. But it is now clear that that is simply not true. . . . Several dozen detainees have been sent home after being held for as long as two years, and none were charged with any offense.

A substantial number of the detainees were arrested by governments in places as remote from Afghanistan as Gambia, in West Africa, turned over to American authorities, and taken to Guantanamo. So it appears from a brief filed in the U.S. Supreme Court in January [2004] by 175 members of the British Parliament. The brief describes what was known about nine British subjects and two others with British connections who were being held in Guantanamo.

British Detainees

One of the British citizens, Asif Iqbal, lived in Tipton, in the British Midlands. His parents, who came to England from Pakistan decades ago, went to Pakistan in July 2001 to find a bride for him. Iqbal, who was 20, followed in September. The marriage was arranged, and he told his parents that he was going to the city of Karachi to meet friends. He telephoned them from there—and was not heard from again.

Two friends of Iqbal's from Tipton followed him to Pakistan in 2001—and similarly disappeared. The brief said they all were apparently seized in unknown circumstances in Pakistan and turned over to Northern Alliance forces [allies of the United States] in Afghanistan. The Northern Alliance in turn handed the three to American forces, who were offering cash rewards for possible terrorists.

Jamal Udeen, 35, a web designer, lived in Manchester, England. His parents had moved there from Jamaica. In 2001 Udeen was, he said, traveling through Afghanistan to Iran when Taliban soldiers saw his British passport and accused him of being a spy. He was taken to a prison in Kandahar and tortured. British officials found him and said he would be sent home, but he was sent to Guantanamo instead.

Martin Mubanga is the son of a former Zambian official who moved to Britain in the 1970s. He was arrested, also for unknown reasons, in Zambia in 2002, turned over to U.S. agents, and taken to Guantanamo.

The brief that describes the British detainees is a remarkable document. It concerns one aspect of the Guantanamo detentions: the determination of the Bush administration to keep the prisoners from having their situations reviewed by any court. The Third Geneva Convention, which the United States has signed and ratified, provides that an independent "competent tribunal" must decide any dispute about a prisoner's status—whether he is, for example, a regular prisoner of war or something unlawful such as a spy or terrorist. The administration declined to follow this convention and declared unilaterally that everyone held in Guantanamo was an "unlawful combatant," not entitled to the rights of a prisoner of war.

The right of a prisoner to challenge his detention before a tribunal of the kind required by the Geneva Convention is not a legal abstraction. It has acute human consequences. That became clear when the United States, at the end of January [2004], released three teenagers who had been held in Guantanamo for more than a year. One of them, 15-year-old Muhammad Ismail Agha, was interviewed on his return to Afghanistan. He said he was looking for work in 2002 when he was arrested by militiamen and turned over to American forces. His family did not know what had happened to him; it was 10 months before he was able to send them a letter from Guantanamo. "He was innocent," a cousin of Agha's said, "and kept in prison all this time."

When some of the prisoners brought legal actions for habeas corpus—the ancient writ that allows anyone imprisoned to test the legality of his detention—the Bush administration argued that federal courts could not hear the case because Guantanamo is outside U.S. sovereignty. Though the United States has complete control of the area under a perpetual treaty with Cuba, a lower court agreed with the administration. But then, in something of a surprise, the U.S. Supreme Court [in] November [2003] agreed to consider the habeas corpus issue. It did so despite a warning from the Justice Department that this was not the court's business but should be left to the president to decide as commander in chief.

It was Guantanamo that led Lord Steyn to speak out about wartime civil liberties in a lecture [in] fall [2003]. It was a remarkable speech from a sitting judge, passionate in its condemnation of the U.S. policy. "As matters stand at present," he said, "the United States courts would refuse to hear a prisoner at Guantanamo Bay who produces credible medical evidence that he has been and is being tortured. They would refuse to hear prisoners who assert that they were not combatants at all."

There is no reason to believe that Guantanamo prisoners have been tortured in, say, the horrifying ways that Saddam Hussein used in Iraq. On the other hand, endless interrogation, isolation, and harsh conditions of confinement are said by medical experts to take a heavy psychological toll. At least 21 prisoners have attempted suicide.

The Threat to U.S. Citizens

Americans may feel safe from the tactics used in John Ashcroft's sweep after 9/11 and in Guantanamo, but they are not. The Bush administration has used similar methods against U.S. citizens, and its lawyers argue that citizens have no greater protection of their freedom. Two citizens have been held without trial for more than 20 months, imprisoned in solitary confinement in Navy brigs, subjected to unending interrogation, and denied the right to consult lawyers. In

January [2004], the U.S. Supreme Court agreed to decide whether the administration has the power it claims to detain citizens without trial.

One of the American detainees, Yaser Esam Hamdi, was seized in Afghanistan during the war there. He was in Guantanamo until it was learned that he was born in Louisiana and is hence an American citizen, whereupon he was moved to the United States. President Bush declared Hamdi an "enemy combatant" and ordered him held indefinitely.

A federal public defender, Frank Dunham, acting on behalf of Hamdi's father, sought Hamdi's release on a writ of habeas corpus. The U.S. Court of Appeals for the 4th Circuit, in Richmond, Virginia, held that the president had the power he claimed when a citizen was found, like Hamdi, on or near a foreign battlefield. The court said specifically that it was not deciding what the president could do with someone arrested inside this country. [On October 9, 2004, Hamdi was released and deported to Saudi Arabia.]

That is the case of Jose Padilla. He was born in Brooklyn, was a gang member, and served several jail terms. In prison he converted to Islam. In May 2002, federal agents arrested him at O'Hare Airport in Chicago and took him to New York as a material witness before a grand jury looking into the 9/11 attack. A judge appointed a lawyer to represent him. But then the Justice Department declared him to be an "enemy combatant" and transferred him to a military brig in South Carolina. His court-appointed lawyer was not allowed to see him after that.

In the Padilla case, a federal trial judge said the government had to show "some evidence" for its description of him as an enemy combatant. The evidence was a statement by a Pentagon official, not subject to cross-examination and without any firsthand witnesses to anything Padilla had allegedly done. The judge said that was enough to satisfy him that there were adequate grounds for his detention.

But on December 18, a panel of the U.S. Court of Appeals for the 2nd Circuit, in New York, rejected that claim by a vote of 2 to 1. Even the dissenter said Padilla should be allowed to consult counsel and argue against his designation as an enemy combatant. The administration has taken this decision to the Supreme Court.

The administration has argued that in the Padilla case, any visit by a lawyer might hurt the process of interrogation by destroying the necessary "atmosphere of dependency and trust between the subject and interrogator." In other words, it might inhibit the effort to overbear the detainee's will. It is precisely because a prisoner alone in the hands of his jailers may be overborne that we have the Miranda rule in the criminal law and the constitutional guarantee of the right to counsel.

Another noteworthy point in the story of Jose Padilla is the way that it was brought before the public. Attorney General Ashcroft, who happened to be in Moscow at the time, made an announcement on television on June 10, 2002. "We have captured a known terrorist," he said. "While in Afghanistan and Pakistan, [he] trained with the enemy. In

apprehending [him] we have disrupted an unfolding terrorist plot to attack the United States by exploding a radioactive 'dirty bomb.'"
Ashcroft thus publicly convicted Padilla without a trial. Any prosecutor
who so grossly prejudiced a defendant would be called to account for
his ethics. [On March 1, 2005, a federal judge in South Carolina ruled
that the United States cannot hold Padilla without charging him.]

Both in the Padilla case and that of Yaser Hamdi, the administration claimed the right to decide on its own not only the law, but the
facts. It asserted the legal power to detain American citizens without
any specific congressional authorization, and it argued for habeas corpus proceedings so narrow that the detainees had no real ability to
contest the finding that they were enemy combatants. Again, the administration claim runs counter to the American idea of government
under law—in particular that it is the courts that decide the facts of
legal issues, not the executive.

The Bush administration has often been charged with unilateral-
ism abroad, notably in its rush to war on Iraq without the support of
the United Nations. The Hamdi and Padilla cases show that it is just
as determined to act unilaterally when it wants to at home, even if
the most profound rights of Americans are overridden.

The attempt to avoid any meaningful review by the courts is especially alarming. Judges are the last line of defense for citizens against
abuse of government power. The British parliamentarians' brief in the
Supreme Court makes the point well. "The United Kingdom and the
United States share an unshakeable commitment to the rule of law," it
says. "Recourse to an independent and impartial tribunal is required
by the rule of law, especially when the justification for detention is
contested or uncertain. Independent judicial review is the product of
over three centuries of constitutional development in both our countries. . . . [We] respectfully submit that this Court should preserve the
judiciary's vital role to insure that executive actions violate neither
the Constitution of the United States nor the international rule of law
and human rights."

The British lawmakers' interest in the Guantanamo situation raises
a question: Why are they so much more concerned about this abuse
of rights than we are? If someone tried to file a similar brief on behalf
of members of the U.S. Congress, he would have little chance of finding 175 senators and representatives willing to sign it. There is not
much public outcry about the Bush administration's attacks on civil
liberties. The press has only latterly begun to pay serious attention.

It is not that the British are more sensitive about these matters.
Hardly. Lord Steyn, in his lecture, mentioned a dark time in Britain's
history. In World War II, the British government detained nearly
27,000 people in Britain as suspect aliens, some of them German Jews
who had found refuge in Britain—and the courts did nothing to hold
the government to rational standards.

Fear of Terrorism

The basic reason for the lack of American public response now must be fear. Fear has brought repression before in U.S. history. It led to savage prison sentences in World War I for people who criticized President Wilson's policies. It led to President Roosevelt's removing 120,000 people of Japanese descent from their homes on the West Coast and confining them in desert camps during World War II.

Americans were traumatized by the attacks of September 11. We felt more vulnerable than we had in living memory. And the truth is that there was more reason to fear further terrorist outrages than there was to think free speech would injure the war effort in 1917 or to fear disloyalty by Japanese Americans in 1942. In times of fear and stress— the times mentioned by Lord Steyn—we want to put ourselves in the hands of a leader. That means the president.

What is especially dangerous about the present fear is that it has no visible time limit. We cannot imagine the "war on terror" coming to a defined end, as the two world wars did. The terrorists are not going to surrender.

President Bush chose to define the struggle against terrorism after September 11 as a war. It might have been better described as a worldwide law enforcement effort against a criminal gang. But the idea of war has stuck, and that makes the need for watchfulness against abuse of power the more acute. If we allow our liberties to be trampled, as is rightly said, the terrorists will have won. The great American contribution to political theory has been the idea of a government of laws, not men. We rely on the law to protect our system of government and our freedom. We abandon that faith in the law at our peril.

The president of the Israeli Supreme Court, Ahron Barak, a judge much respected around the world, has addressed the subject of terror and the law. He speaks from experience, given Israel's unending struggle with terrorism.

"Terrorism does not justify the neglect of accepted legal norms," Justice Barak wrote in 2002. "This is how we distinguish ourselves from the terrorists themselves. They act against the law, by violating and trampling it, while in its war against terrorism, a democratic state acts within the framework of the law and according to the law. It is, therefore, not merely a war of the state against its enemies; it is also a war of the Law against its enemies."

AN ARAB AMERICAN DEFENDS RACIAL PROFILING

Rob Asghar

Racial profiling will make the United States a safer society, according to Rob Asghar, a Pakistani American writer and editor. In the following personal account, Asghar describes how, on a recent flight, he was able to move unimpeded through security at Los Angeles International Airport, even though he fit the very profile of a terrorist tied to al Qaeda: a young, bearded, South Asian male traveling alone. By not stopping him, Asghar writes, airport officials were making air travel less safe for all passengers. Asghar exhorts other Americans with ethnicities similar to his own to graciously tolerate a limited amount of racial profiling in the interest of national security.

It's time for some ethnic profiling.

A few weeks ago, my mother and father returned to Southern California after a long stay in their native Pakistan. Spotting me outside LAX's international terminal, my mother rushed up to hug me when she noticed something different about me: a goatee. "Get rid of that!" she said with typical maternal sensitivity that knows no geographical or cultural bounds. I responded, "But, Mom, I like it. Kinda makes me look dangerous!" She groaned, "Yes. You'll never get on an airplane again."

I laughed, but then wondered whether she had a point, especially since I'd soon be visiting my baby niece in Michigan. When the day arrived for my flight to Detroit, I showed up at Los Angeles International Airport wearing an Old Navy flag shirt and would have happily sported an "I carry no weapons" baseball cap if such an item were manufactured. To my surprise, I sailed through. Maybe I can't get arrested in this town, or in my destination city, or in connecting cities. At the check-in desks and six different checkpoints, no one batted an eye at me. Relief soon turned to irritation. Here, after all, was a youngish South Asian male traveling alone. My driver's license could easily have belonged to another person, revealing as it did a clean-shaven person with (lamentably) a fuller head of hair than the man

Rob Asghar, "A Show of Grace for Safety's Sake," *Los Angeles Times,* July 6, 2002.

standing before them. By giving me an easy ride through security, the airport staff was making me—and every other traveler—much less safe.

Profiling in Pakistan

I recalled the last time I had facial hair, a dozen years ago, during which time I traveled to Pakistan. Security staff in L.A. and London sped me along, but their counterparts in Islamabad were relentless and overbearingly cautious in ensuring that the guy with the beard was the same fellow as the unbearded person pictured in my passport. I almost didn't make my flight back to L.A. because the Pakistani police were so intent on stopping anyone trying to get to the United States illegally.

Why the difference in approach? The American and British security personnel may have overlooked me because we "all look the same." But more likely, the Pakistani personnel were less squeamish about ethnically profiling one of their own.

Racial and ethnic profiling can be repugnant. But they also represent a sensible aspect of human logic, tied to what social psychologists would consider a normal cognitive process called "sampling bias." Some groups should be watched in certain benign ways.

We, the watched, have to be ready to respond with grace to real and perceived slights, whenever and wherever they may happen. Middle Eastern Christians can look to a Christ who calls on them to turn the other cheek. Muslims can look to a prophet Muhammad who was long-suffering and merciful toward Meccan authorities who had abused him during his ministry. The most compelling force on Earth is the power unleashed by the person who can take a hit with grace. And most important, a degree of sensitively handled racial profiling will make the U.S. a safer society. So stop strip-searching the little old white lady and take another gander at me the next time I come walking through LAX.

"Grow up, and that is a terribly hard thing to do," F. Scott Fitzgerald said. "It is much easier to skip it and go from one childhood to another." Good counsel for profiling-phobic Transportation Secretary Norman Y. Mineta and others in this nation who may be overly sensitive about profiling. In coming years, all of us will need to show the maturity that can more graciously accommodate the small and large insults of life.

THE HARMS OF RACIAL PROFILING

Dan B. Gerson

Before the attacks of September 11, 2001, racial profiling affected primarily African Americans. After the terrorist attacks, the case for racial profiling changed dramatically. The following selection by Dan B. Gerson recounts the harrowing saga of Nacer and Fahti Mustafa, two U.S. citizens who attempted to travel by air shortly after the terrorist attacks. That the men were of the same racial and ethnic background as the Middle Eastern terrorists resulted in their detention by airport authorities. Gerson writes that the men had not engaged in any criminal activity and that their subsequent prosecution and incarceration—one was jailed for sixty-seven days—was predicated on nothing other than their Middle Eastern ethnicity. Gerson is an attorney in Houston, Texas.

On September 15, 2001, two Middle Eastern men, sixty-seven-year-old Fahti Mustafa and his son, twenty-four-year-old Nacer Mustafa, traveled by air from Leon, Mexico, to Bush Intercontinental Airport in Houston, Texas, en route to their home in Florida. They had gone to Mexico on September 9 in order to purchase leather and other dry goods to be resold in Fahti Mustafa's dry goods store located in their hometown of Labelle, Florida, a small agricultural town. Fahti Mustafa, a Palestinian-American who became a United States citizen in 1972, took Nacer, who is also a United States citizen, having been born in Puerto Rico, along with him to help because Fahti is very hard of hearing and suffers from other medical problems, including diabetes and heart disease.

Alleged Passport Problems

The father and son were originally scheduled to return to Florida on September 13, but due to the emergency shutdown of air travel following the terrorist attacks of September 11 were unable to travel until the 15th. The Mustafas landed in Houston and presented their United States passports to immigration authorities. An INS [Immigration and Naturalization Service] officer thought that he saw something suspicious about the passports and called in an FBI agent, who, after detaining the Mustafas, summoned an agent of the State Department Diplomatic Service, which is in charge of passport matters. The State Department agent, who also happened to be part of the Gulf Coast Terrorist Task Force, concluded that each passport, although issued at separate locations and dates, had been altered by the placing of an extra layer of laminate over the existing laminate. Both Mustafas, after being taken to separate rooms and questioned, denied any knowledge of improprieties regarding their passports. The agent, Christopher Culver, tried to get Nacer to admit that he had altered his passport and asked to which country he would like to go if deported. Nacer told the agent that he was a United States citizen, but that information did not seem to make an impression on the agent. A criminal complaint was filed against both Mustafas alleging that they were in possession of altered passports.

In the complaint, Agent Culver swore that the passports "had obviously been altered with the introduction of an additional clear sheet on top of the genuine laminate." He explained how altered passports can be used to aid terrorist activity and drug-smuggling organizations. The agent attempted to cast the Mustafas in the worst light, stating that, when questioned, "The Mustafas declined to offer any explanation," when in fact they denied knowledge of any alterations. He suggested that no records were available regarding Fahti's naturalization, and characterized Nacer's nickname and family name as "aliases."

Detention

Both Mustafas were placed in the Federal Detention Center in Houston, Texas. The assistant United States attorney handling the case requested that both Mustafas be detained without bail as flight risks because of "national security." The pre-trial services officer, in this relatively minor case that would ordinarily result in a sentence of approximately six months incarceration or probation, recommended detention. At the detention hearing, Agent Culver, although admitting that he had no evidence linking either Mustafa to terrorism, expanded his earlier allegations and showed the magistrate judge where the passport had been taken apart and resewn. He also repeated to the court how altered passports can be used to aid terrorism and drug smuggling. In court the Mustafas presented records and witnesses that showed that they were stable citizens of their county. The judge considered everything about the Mustafas suspicious: the fact that both father and son had traveled to the Middle East; the year that Nacer graduated high school; whether or not Fahti was retired or operated a business. The whole process was skewed against the Mustafas in light of the events of September 11. They were definitely not being afforded the presumption of innocence even though none of the September 11 hijackers were Palestinian and none were United States citizens. Following the hearing, and after eleven days in jail, Fahti was released (just barely). He was required to wear an electronic leg monitor and to remain under a curfew that amounted to a virtual home arrest, allowing him to go to work during the day. The next day, Fahti, in ill health, hard of hearing, and speaking poor English, afraid to get on an airplane, took a bus home to Florida.

The magistrate, in a scathing detention order, denied Nacer bond and detained him as a flight risk and a possible threat to national security. This is a man that lives in the same small town as his parents, operates his own filling station, has a wife and two small children, and whose only conviction was a misdemeanor probation for assault that he lived out. Nacer immediately appealed the magistrate's detention order. The district judge wrote an even more harsh opinion upholding the detention. In it he questioned how a small store-owner could afford to travel to the Middle East and cited the aliases and false birth dates and social security numbers that Nacer had allegedly used in the past. Apparently some law enforcement officer had written down his date of birth and social security number with one digit off or transposed; and as stated before, his "aliases" were his nickname "Victor" and his mother's last name.

Nacer sat in the Federal Detention Center for sixty-seven days, far from home, missing his family, locked up in his own country, and charged with an offense for which he was totally innocent. Shortly before the case was set for trial, the assistant United States attorney received a scientific report from the INS lab that showed that there was no evidence that the two passports had been tampered with or altered. The cases were dismissed and Nacer Mustafa was let out of the Federal Detention Center. He received no explanation and no apology, he just walked out. Both Nacer and Fahti filed petitions under the Hyde Amendment, requesting that the government reimburse them for reasonable attorney's fees because they had been wrongfully prosecuted. In order to collect money from the government under the Hyde Amendment, the prevailing defendant must show that the government's actions were "frivolous, vexatious, or in bad faith." We claimed that Agent Culver's assertions that the passports had obviously been resewn and altered were, in fact, frivolous, vexatious, and in bad faith. The same district judge who denied Nacer bail wrote the opinion denying the Hyde Amendment claim, stating that in this time of dire national emergency all parties working for the government acted "in the utmost good faith."

Altered Lives

That is the end of the legal saga of Fahti and Nacer Mustafa, but their lives have been altered by what they have gone through. Nacer wonders what his customers and neighbors are thinking when he speaks to them, feeling that perhaps he is under suspicion even though everyone knows that the charges were dropped. He keeps the dismissal papers handy to show people if they are interested or curious. Nacer maintains a lower profile than before and is a little more guarded, refraining from loud conversations and debates with his friends and family when out in public. Fahti has gone through a heart bypass operation since his release, and, according to Nacer, sometimes just sits and stares into space. The hardest thing, says Nacer, was hearing his father in the next cell, crying. "This man has never even had a parking ticket, and he loves this country, but we were innocent, and look what they did to us."

Unlike the hundreds of Middle Eastern men who were detained indefinitely after September 11, held in secret without criminal charges or due process of law, the Mustafas were given due process. However, due process did them little good when all parties involved, including the arresting agent, the pre-trial services officer, the federal prosecutor, the magistrates, and the district judges took the worst view of the Mustafas and concluded that they were a risk to national security. Both men were incarcerated, humiliated, prosecuted, and forced to spend a large amount of money to defend themselves . . . collateral damage in the war against terrorism.

ORGANIZATIONS TO CONTACT

American Civil Liberties Union (ACLU)
125 Broad St., 18th Fl., New York, NY 10004-2400
(212) 549-2500 • fax: (212) 549-2646
e-mail: aclu@aclu.org • Web site: www.aclu.org
The ACLU is a national organization that works to defend civil rights as guaranteed in the Constitution. It publishes various materials on civil liberties, including the triannual newsletter *Civil Liberties* and a set of handbooks on individual rights.

Americans United for Separation of Church and State (AUSCS)
518 C St. NE, Washington, DC 20002
(202) 466-3234 • fax: (202) 466-2587
e-mail: americansunited@au.org • Web site: www.au.org
AUSCS works to protect religious freedom for all Americans. Its principal means of action are litigation, education, and advocacy. It opposes the passing of either federal or state laws that threaten the separation of church and state. Its publications include brochures, pamphlets, and the monthly newsletter *Church and State*.

Cato Institute
1000 Massachusetts Ave. NW, Washington, DC 20001-5403
(202) 842-0200 • fax: (202) 842-3490
e-mail: cato@cato.org • Web site: www.cato.org
The Cato Institute is a libertarian public policy research foundation. It advocates limited government and strongly opposes regulations on speech. The institute distributes books, policy papers, reports, and the triannual *Cato Journal*.

Center for Democracy and Technology (CDT)
1634 Eye St. NW, Washington, DC 20006
(202) 637-9800 • fax: (202) 637-0968
e-mail: feedback@cdt.org • Web site: www.cdt.org
CDT's mission is to develop public policy solutions that advance constitutional civil liberties and democratic values in new computer and communications media. Its publications include issue briefs, policy papers, and *CDT Policy Posts*, an online publication that covers issues regarding the civil liberties of people using the information superhighway.

Electronic Frontier Foundation (EFF)
454 Shotwell St., San Francisco, CA 94110
(415) 436-9333 • fax: (415) 436-9993
e-mail: ask@eff.org • Web site: www.eff.org
EFF works to protect privacy and freedom of expression in the arena of computers and the Internet. Its missions include supporting litigation that protects First Amendment rights. EFF's Web site publishes an electronic bulletin, *Effector*, and the guidebook *Protecting Yourself Online: The Definitive Resource on Safety, Freedom, and Privacy in Cyberspace*.

Freedom Forum
1101 Wilson Blvd., Arlington, VA 22209
(703) 528-0800 • fax: (703) 284-3770
e-mail: news@freedomforum.org • Web site: www.freedomforum.org

The Freedom Forum is a national organization that works to protect free speech and freedom of the press. It monitors developments in media and First Amendment issues on its Web site. The forum's First Amendment Center focuses on the study and exploration of free-expression issues. It publishes the annual report "State of the First Amendment," the teacher's guide *Free Speech and Music*, the report *Violence and the Media: An Exploration of Cause, Effect, and the First Amendment*, and other studies and briefing papers.

Heritage Foundation
214 Massachusetts Ave. NE, Washington, DC 20002-4999
(202) 546-4400 • fax: (202) 544-8328
e-mail: info@heritage.org • Web site: www.heritage.org

The foundation is a conservative public policy organization dedicated to free-market principles, individual liberty, and limited government. It favors limiting freedom of the press when that freedom threatens national security. Its resident scholars publish position papers on a wide range of issues through publications such as the weekly *Backgrounder* and the quarterly *Policy Review*.

Human Rights Watch
350 Fifth Ave., 34th Fl., New York, NY 10118-3299
(212) 290-4700 • fax: (212) 736-1300
e-mail: hrwnyc@hrw.org • Web site: www.hrw.org

Human Rights Watch regularly investigates human rights abuses in more than seventy countries around the world. It promotes civil liberties and defends freedom of thought, due process, and equal protection of the law. Its goal is to hold governments accountable for human rights violations they may commit against individuals because of their political, ethnic, or religious affiliations. It publishes the *Human Rights Watch Quarterly Newsletter*, the annual *Human Rights Watch World Report*, and a semiannual publications catalog.

Morality in Media (MIM)
475 Riverside Dr., Suite 239, New York, NY 10115
(212) 870-3222 • fax: (212) 870-2765
e-mail: mim@moralityinmedia.org • Web site: www.moralityinmedia.org

Morality in Media is an interfaith organization that fights pornography and opposes indecency in the mainstream media. It maintains the National Obscenity Law Center, a clearinghouse of legal materials on obscenity law. MIM publishes the bimonthlies *Morality in Media* and *Obscenity Law Bulletin* and several reports, including *Minors' Access to Pornography on the Internet Though Library and School Computers*.

National Coalition Against Censorship (NCAC)
275 Seventh Ave., New York, NY 10001
(212) 807-6222 • fax: (212) 807-6245
e-mail: ncac@ncac.org • Web site: www.ncac.org

NCAC is an alliance of organizations committed to defending freedom of thought, inquiry, and expression by engaging in public education and advocacy on national and local levels. It publishes periodic reports and the quarterly *Censorship News*.

National Coalition for the Protection of Children & Families (NCPCF)
800 Compton Rd., Suite 9224, Cincinnati, OH 45231-9964
(513) 521-6227 • fax: (513) 521-6337
Web site: www.nationalcoalition.org

NCPCF is an organization of business, religious, and civic leaders who work to eliminate pornography. Because it believes a link exists between pornography and violence, NCPCF encourages citizens to support the enforcement of obscenity laws and to close down pornography outlets in their neighborhoods. Publications include the booklets *It's Not Your Fault: The One You Love Uses Porn, Sex Addiction: Too Much of a Good Thing*, and *Warning: What You Risk by Using Porn.*

People for the American Way Foundation (PFAW)
2000 M St. NW, Suite 400, Washington, DC 20036
(202) 467-4999 • fax: (202) 293-2672
e-mail: pfaw@pfaw.org • Web site: www.pfaw.org

PFAW works to increase tolerance and respect for America's diverse cultures, religions, and values. It distributes educational materials, leaflets, and brochures, including the reports *A Right Wing and a Prayer: The Religious Right in Your Public Schools* and *Attacks on the Freedom to Learn.*

Religion and Public Education Resource Center (RPERC)
239 Trinity Hall, Chico, CA 95929-0740
(530) 898-4739
e-mail: bgrelle@csuchico.edu • Web site: www.csuchico.edu

The center believes religion should be studied in public schools in ways that do not promote the values or beliefs of one religion over another but that expose students to such beliefs. It publishes the triannual magazine *Religion and Public Education* and resource materials for teachers and administrators.

Rockford Institute Center on Religion and Society
934 N. Main St., Rockford, IL 61103
(815) 964-5053 • fax: (815) 965-1826
e-mail: rkfdinst@bossnt.com

The center is a research and educational organization that advocates a more public role for religion and religious values in American life. It publishes the quarterly *This World: A Journal of Religion and Public Life* and the monthly *Religion and Society Report.*

BIBLIOGRAPHY

Books

Lee C. Bollinger and Geoffrey R. Stone, eds.   *Must We Defend Nazis? Hate Speech, Pornography, and the First Amendment.* Chicago: University of Chicago Press, 2002.

Tammy Bruce   *The New Thought Police: Inside the Left's Assault on Free Speech and Free Minds.* Roseville, CA: Forum, 2001.

David Cole   *Enemy Aliens: Double Standards and Constitutional Freedoms in the War on Terrorism.* New York: New Press, 2003.

Kenneth R. Craycraft   *American Myth of Religious Freedom.* Dallas: Spence, 2003.

Thomas Curry   *Farewell to Christendom: The Future of Church and State in America.* New York: Oxford University Press, 2001.

Michael Kent Curtis   *Free Speech, "The People's Darling Privilege": Struggles for Freedom of Expression in American History.* Durham and London: Duke University Press, 2000.

Alan Dershowitz   *Rights from Wrongs: A Secular Theory of the Origins of Rights.* New York: Basic Books, 2004.

Daniel L. Dreisbach   *Thomas Jefferson and the Wall of Separation Between Church and State.* New York: New York University Press, 2003.

Stanley Fish   *There's No Such Thing as Free Speech: And It's a Good Thing, Too.* New York: Oxford University Press, 1994.

John B. Harer and Eugenia E. Harrell   *People for and Against Unrestricted Expression.* Westport, CT: Greenwood, 2002.

Marjorie Heins   *Not in Front of the Children: "Indecency," Censorship, and the Innocence of Youth.* New York: Hill and Wang, 2001.

Nat Hentoff   *The War on the Bill of Rights and the Gathering Resistance.* New York: Seven Stories Press, 2003.

Kathryn Kolbert and Zak Mettger   *Censoring the Web.* New York: New Press, 2001.

Milton Ridvas Konvitz   *Fundamental Liberties of a Free People: Religion, Speech, Press, Assembly.* Somerset, NJ: Transaction, 2003.

Richard Leone and Greg Anrig, eds.   *The War on Our Freedoms: Civil Liberties in an Age of Terrorism.* New York: Century Foundation, 2003.

Judith Levine   *Harmful to Minors: The Perils of Protecting Children from Sex.* Minneapolis: University of Minnesota Press, 2002.

Leonard W. Levy   *Origins of the Bill of Rights.* New Haven, CT: Yale University Press, 1999.

John T. Noonan and Edward McGlynn Gaffney	*Religious Freedom: History, Cases, and Other Materials on the Interaction of Religion and Government.* New York: Foundation Press, 2001.
Christian Parenti	*The Soft Cage: Surveillance in America from Slavery to the War on Terror.* New York: Basic Books, 2003.
Robert S. Peck	*Libraries, the First Amendment, and Cyberspace: What You Need to Know.* Chicago: American Library Association, 2000.
William Rehnquist	*All the Laws but One: Civil Liberties in Wartime.* New York: Vintage Books, 2000.
Jeffrey Rosen	*The Naked Crowd: Reclaiming Security and Freedom in an Anxious Age.* New York: Random House, 2004.
Nadine Strossen	*Defending Pornography: Free Speech, Sex, and the Fight for Women's Rights.* New York: New York University Press, 2000.
Jonathan D. Wallace	*Sex, Law, and Cyberspace: Freedom and Censorship on the Frontiers of the Online Revolution.* New York: Owl Books, 1997.

Periodicals

John Ashcroft	"Is the Patriot Act Worth Keeping? It's a Strong Tool Against Terror," *Milwaukee Journal Sentinel*, October 25, 2003.
William Beaver	"The Dilemma of Internet Pornography," *Business and Society Review*, Fall 2000.
Robert Bork	"The Sanctity of Smut," *Wall Street Journal*, April 27, 2004.
Andrew Brown	"The Limits of Freedom," *New Statesman*, February 12, 1999.
Matthew Brzezinski	"Fortress America," *New York Times Magazine*, February 23, 2003.
CQ Researcher	"Civil Liberties in Wartime," December 14, 2001.
Valerie Demmer	"Civil Liberties and Homeland Security," *Humanist*, January/February 2002.
Barbara Dority	"Your Every Move," *Humanist*, January/February 2004.
C. Gearty	"Terror, Human Rights, and Civil Liberties: Authoritarian Answers," *World Today*, August/September 2003.
Onkar Ghate	"Professor Ward Churchill, the First Amendment, and Free Speech on Campus," *Capitalism Magazine*, February 15, 2005.
Allen Jayne	"Jefferson's Philosophical Wall of Separation," *Humanist*, January 1999.
Roger Kimball	"The Case for Censorship," *Wall Street Journal*, October 8, 2000.

Heather Mac Donald   "Straight Talk on Homeland Security," *City Journal*, Summer 2003.

Kenan Malik   "Protect the Freedom to Shock," *New Statesman*, August 13, 2001.

Ed Morgan   "Terrorism Challenges the Profiling Taboo," *National Post*, January 2, 2002.

Deborah Pearlstein   "Criminal Justice and the Erosion of Rights," *American Prospect*, October 1, 2004.

Riad Saloojee   "Why We Must Say No to Profiling," *Globe and Mail*, June 10, 2002.

Stephen J. Schulhofer   "At War with Liberty: Post 9/11, Due Process and Security Have Taken a Beating," *American Prospect*, March 1, 2003.

Max J. Skidmore   "Censorship: Who Needs It? How the Conventional Wisdom Restricts Information's Free Flow," *Journal of Popular Culture*, Winter 2001.

Steve Steinke   "Insubstantial Privacy Losses," *Network Magazine*, August 4, 2002.

Erika Waak   "The Global Reach of Privacy Invasion," *Humanist*, November/December 2002.

Jonathan D. Wallace   "Preserving Anonymity of the Internet," *USA Today*, November 2000.

Allison Weisberg   "John Ashcroft and Civil Liberties," FrontPage Magazine.com, February 3, 2003.

Jay Winik   "Security Before Freedom," *Wall Street Journal*, October 23, 2001.

Jonathan Yardley   "Read No Evil: A Textbook Case of Censorship," *Washington Post*, June 12, 2003.

INDEX